THE IDEA OF A COLLEGE

THE IDEA

OF A COLLEGE

BY

ELTON TRUEBLOOD

PROFESSOR OF PHILOSOPHY

EARLHAM COLLEGE

HARPER & BROTHERS PUBLISHERS

NEW YORK

Library of Congress catalog card number: 59–11562

Dedicated

to

EDWARD F. GALLAHUE

who has

provided new

conveniences for study

CONTENTS

PREFACE

The current debate concerning education is not a temporary feature of the American scene. It will continue, not because we love to argue about public affairs, but because, deep in our heritage, is the conviction that the good life cannot be maintained apart from the production of excellent schools and colleges. The debate about education is inevitable, but it cannot be really fruitful unless concerned citizens go beyond mere condemnation to the elaboration of an ideal in the light of which current and future achievements may be judged. What is needed, at this point in the discussion, is primary emphasis upon educational purposes. We shall not be able to proceed intelligently, in trying to answer questions concerning means, until we are far more clear about fundamental ends.

The present volume is devoted to one phase of this subject, that of higher education at the college level. It began with a single address before the Association of American Colleges, which the Association published in its *Bulletin* and as a separate reprint.[1] This address was called "The Idea of a College," and there seems to be no good reason why we should not keep the same title for the fuller treatment of the subject. The value of the title lies in the fact that it reminds literate readers of an important book produced by Cardinal Newman a little more than a century ago, *The Idea of a University*. External conditions have changed, but the essential purpose of higher education has altered little in the

[1] *Association of American Colleges Bulletin*, Vol. XXXVI, No. 1, March 1950, pp. 29–36.

intervening years. What we seek is still "the force, the steadiness, the comprehensiveness and the versatility of intellect, the command over our own powers, the instinctive just estimate of things as they pass before us, which sometimes indeed is a natural gift, but commonly is not gained without much effort and the exercise of years." This ideal is so good and so important that we shall, if we are wise, combine all of the thought of which we are capable in the effort to embody it in a form appropriate to the life of the twentieth century.

The reader, as he proceeds with this volume, will have ample evidence of the ways in which not merely Cardinal Newman but Professor Whitehead and scores of others have helped in the task of clarifying problems and reaching conclusions. Among the American voices that have been helpful, Woodrow Wilson's is perhaps the clearest of all. We realize that we do not need to go abroad, in order to find an adequate statement of our educational philosophy, when we read again Wilson's words. Speaking of the difference which a college should try to make in the lives of students, he said, "It should give them elasticity of faculty and breadth of vision, so that they shall have a surplus of mind to expend, not upon their profession only, for its liberalization and enlargement, but also upon the broader interests which lie about them." The problem which has given rise to this book is the problem of how this "surplus of mind" is to be produced.

Though some of the intellectual indebtedness is indicated in footnotes and in the concluding Bibliography, these do not tell all. Living all of his mature life in or near colleges and universities, the author has learned from his colleagues and his students as well as from books. He has abundant reason for gratitude.

ELTON TRUEBLOOD

Earlham College
February 1959

THE IDEA OF A COLLEGE

I

The College in America

"It is the object of learning, not only to satisfy the curiosity and perfect the spirits of individual men, but also to advance civilization."
WOODROW WILSON

THE human mind does not work at its best in isolation. There are times when the creative thinker, in order to function most perfectly, must seek solitude, but such solitude is valuable only because it is not continuous. Thought may be developed in solitude, but, in normal experience, it is not aroused except in community. Though we speak much of self-reliance, the truth is that we need each other, not only in the application of ideas, but even more in the inception of ideas; for, though minds are stimulated in various ways, their chief source of stimulation is other minds. The intellectual life grows in a variety of ways, but its most nourishing soil is that of a fellowship of minds.

It is out of the need for intellectual community that the idea of a college has developed. We have, slowly and laboriously, sought to create artificial situations in which the powers of men can be developed rapidly and by calculated means. We have labored to construct societies of various levels, intended to facilitate and to preserve the civilizing process. In the experience of Socrates and his students the fellowship was both spontaneous and evanescent,

1

but with Plato it took relatively permanent form. The college as we know it includes much of the teaching of Socrates, but the organization of the academic society is an extension and embodiment of Plato's fertile dream. Civilization is a risky business, which can move rapidly in different directions. It can go down as easily as it can advance. Indeed, a great deal of recorded human history is the story of the decline of once brilliant civilizations. What is the chance that ours will be different in outcome? This is something which we do not know, but we are at least aware that, whether we endure or advance, such endurance or advancement will be achieved only by conscious and imaginative effort. It is intrinsic to the very nature of the human situation that stability is impossible; for if we are not advancing, we are already in decay. While decline is easy, it is not possible to advance without taking thought and without taking thought *together*. The lone thinker is a voice crying in the wilderness; he needs students and teachers and colleagues and helpers if he is to be effective; in short, he needs to be part of a thinking community.

A college may profitably be compared to a pumping station on a pipe line. Nearly all who have traveled near the great pipe lines have noticed that in order to keep the oil moving, pumping stations have to be installed every few miles. This is true even when the line goes downhill, because the natural forces are inadequate. We have to do something about it, and the pumping station is the answer. A college is a pumping station on the pipe line of civilization. It is designed to do what cannot be done naturally or easily. It is a conscious effort to avoid the decay of civilization and to make that civilization worthy of permanence.

That colleges are bound to have an effect upon the outcome of current history is obvious. If we succeed in destroying the race, that will be partly because of what has been developed in colleges; and if we come out into a brighter day, that, too, in part, will be because of what college men and women have thought. Ivory towers are among the most productive of human structures! Men

who are sufficiently advanced in scientific thought to put earth satellites and artificial planets into orbit are likely to think creatively
along other lines, including those of social order and moral
values. A totalitarian government is, therefore, in a hard predicament. It is forced to encourage higher education if it is to achieve
dominance in weapons or in industrial achievement, but this
higher education that is encouraged may include, as essentials of
the process, the seeds of the destruction of the system which
supports it. Knowledge gives power, but it is hard to develop
knowledge without freedom as a by-product.[1]

Because the college is a contrived product, it declines rapidly
and seriously without constant vigilance. In this regard it is like
hybrid seed corn and other products of human imagination, including both flora or fauna, which lose their peculiar excellence
whenever conscious effort is relaxed. The ingrown college, without
help from the outside, would decline as the horses of Chinco-
teague Island have declined. In some places we already see academic decay that is truly shocking. Not only are there high
schools which, in spite of expensive buildings and reasonably good
salaries for teachers, teach no really demanding subjects, but there
are also universities and colleges which grant degrees to graduates
who have almost none of the marks of a genuine education.

Far from lumping all higher education together, we are now
well aware of enormous differences of level. How much is a
Bachelor of Arts degree worth? That depends, for the most part,
upon the nature of the institution which bestows it. In some
colleges such a degree can be had by merely accumulating 120
hours of credit, and this can be accumulated in almost any subjects. In other institutions the degree is not granted unless the

[1] Thus George F. Kennan, speaking of contemporary Russia, says, "By its
admirable programme of popular education, which in many ways deserves our
respect, it has created a new educated class which is simply not prepared to
accept the old devices of Communist thought-control, and is determined to do
its thinking for itself." *Russia, The Atom and The West* (London: Oxford
University Press, 1958), p. 7.

individual shows real competence in a chosen field of concentration and a general level of cultural achievement in areas beyond it. Inequality is one of the most striking features of the academic situation.

Because there is so much inequality and confusion, as well as the danger of a general decline of civilization, it is a matter of first importance to reconsider the whole question of what a college is and what it ought to be. The reason for stressing the college rather than the university is that, in America, the college provides the characteristic and central pattern of higher education. Because this is so, we need to re-examine it in regard to both ends and means.

What we are seeking to understand is something in the nature of a Platonic ideal. For present purposes the universal is far more valuable than is the particular. Each particular institution has its faults, but there is a good chance of correcting these faults, provided the standard is clear and consequently potent. Only by fastening our gaze upon the universal will the particular be altered. In some cases we need to build new colleges, as a consequence of the growth of population; and when this is done, we ought to be careful to profit from all the former academic experience that is available. We must study many societies, as Senator Stanford studied Harvard after it had existed for 250 years, before he was ready to establish the institution which bears the name of his son. Though the delineation of the ideal is needed in establishing new colleges, it is needed even more in regulating, reviving, and guiding old and existing colleges.

The variety exhibited in the higher education of the West is immense. In America alone we have at least six major types of academic establishment. The chief of these are the independent university, the state university, the liberal arts four-year college, the two-year junior college, the municipal, nonresidential college, and the technical institute. The liberal arts college stands near the the middle of this spectrum. It is our characteristic intellectual production, not duplicated in other parts of the West. The chief reason why Europeans have such great difficulty in understanding the American college is that they simply do not have its counterpart. They are mystified when they hear about our students attending institutions which are obviously concerned with important studies, but learning many different things at once in a setting different from either school or university, as these are known to them.

In three hundred years of experience the American college has developed into something that stands in contrast to nearly all European patterns of academic life. It is an intellectual society, usually located alone instead of in clusters after the English plan, and devoted to the general education of persons whose four years of sharing in the enterprise normally include the age period from eighteen to twenty-two. Many, and perhaps the majority, of those who attend do not know, when they enter, what their subject of concentration may be, and they certainly feel uncertain about particular choices of vocation. They attend, characteristically, not because they know what they expect to do, but in the hope that they may find this out, under optimum conditions of intelligent choice.

The college pattern as actually developed in America is substantially similar to that which was elaborated in the fertile imagination of John Milton and described by him in his famous tractate *Of Education*. In this essay he not only outlined a course of general studies, but indicated something of the nature of the academic society which he believed an advancing civilization required. In his treatise Milton concerned himself with liberating studies, with exercise, and with diet, all made possible by a setting described as follows:

First to find out a spacious house and ground about it fit for an academy, and big enough to lodge a hundred and fifty persons, whereof twenty or thereabout may be attendants, all under the government of one, who shall be thought of desert sufficient, and ability either to do all, or wisely to direct, and oversee it done. This place should be at once both school and university, not heeding a remove to any other house of scholarship, except it be some peculiar College of Law, or Physic, where they mean to be practitioners. . . . After this pattern, as many Edifices may be converted to this use, as shall be needful in every city throughout this land, which would tend much to the increase of learning and civility everywhere.

The European university, by contrast to most American institutions, is made up largely of students who enter for a particular purpose, often vocational. Frequently the European students are a little older when they enter than is the characteristic American freshman, because the secondary school has included some of the studies which are beyond those ordinarily pursued in an American high school. A good example of what is expected in attendance at a European university is that provided by Dr. Schweitzer's autobiographical account.

When in 1893, in my nineteenth year, I was preparing for the final examination at the Gymnasium, I was only beginning darkly to suspect what ideas were at work within me to the control of which I should one day have to submit. The claims of the immediate future were for the present supreme. I was looking forward with joy to the life of a University student, and I boldly determined to take up as my subjects philosophy, theology, and music.[2]

The characteristic student at an English university goes to "read" some subject, such as classics or history, and often concentrates on this subject from the beginning. Only a minority of students, however, do this in American universities. Thus the idea of a college is not limited, in America, to institutions which happen to be called colleges, but is found also in the great universities. The majority of the students at Yale or Stanford are attending in essentially the same mood and for the same purposes as though they were attending Oberlin or Amherst. Indeed Yale

[2] Albert Schweitzer, *Memoirs of Childhood and Youth* (New York: The Macmillan Company, 1949), p. 62.

University has, in its reorganization into separate undergraduate colleges, given public recognition to the enduring validity of the college idea. The valuable heritage of Yale College is maintained by the expedient of adding to the number of such colleges, working side by side.

Though most large universities have not as yet followed Yale's lead in this matter, it is important to realize that undergraduate life in most universities is really college life on a large scale. There are state-supported institutions which, in spite of tax support, demonstrate in almost all ways the same pattern that has long been known in the independent liberal arts college. One of the most striking illustrations of this is provided by Miami University at Oxford, Ohio. The majority of undergraduate students experience up to four years of general education. Thus the only parts of what we call universities which are comparable in mood to their European counterparts are the professional graduate schools and the departments concerned with advanced degrees.[3] In short, though we use the term university widely, the college pattern is the chief pattern of academic America. Since, for better or for worse, this is how our intellectual life has developed, our task is to understand this pattern and to glorify it.

The first American colleges were not intended to be essentially different from the English colleges on which they were modeled. Undoubtedly the small institution on the north bank of the Charles River was expected to become, in the New World, something of what John Harvard's College at Cambridge already was. The absence of a cluster of colleges came about, not by principle, but because of the facts of geography. The colleges, as they were founded in succeeding generations, were widely separated according to the needs of a growing and expanding nation. The estab-

[3] The first serious effort on the part of an American institution to provide advanced study in the arts and sciences on the European model was made in the establishment of Johns Hopkins University in 1876. In spite, however, of the eminence of Johns Hopkins in this field, the university still maintains a liberal arts college.

lishment of these many points of potential illumination was actually a fortunate development. Equally fortunate was the unintended production of an institution that is unique in that it is both school and university, in one sense, while in another sense it is neither. This came to pass because it was what the developing nation required. A little over a century ago, Professor William S. Tyler of Amherst College expressed clearly the idea that the American college already exhibited unique features different from those of European institutions. In a pamphlet published in 1857 he wrote:

American colleges bear a general resemblance to the English colleges, from which they spring; not, however, without important modifications, which bring them into nearer conformity to the genius of our institutions, into closer connection with the wants and wishes of the people . . . the people have built them with their own hands, and cherished them in their own hearts. They are the people's colleges. . . . Scarcely anything in America is more distinctively American than the relation between the colleges and the common people.

The close connection between the college and the people was an important feature of American life long before Professor Tyler made his significant observation and was, indeed, one of the controlling factors in building the concept of an independent nation. Widespread respect for learning was clearly recognized by John Adams in a paper written eleven years before the Declaration of Independence. The development of the American mentality was such, he said, that it tended to encourage makers of opinion "to use every measure and take every precaution in their power to propagate and perpetuate knowledge. For this purpose they laid very early the foundations of colleges and invested them with ample privileges and emoluments; and it is remarkable that they have left among their posterity so universal an affection and veneration for those seminaries and for liberal education that the meanest of the people contribute cheerfully to the support and maintenance of them every year. . . . So that the education of all ranks of people was made the care and expense of the public in a manner that I believe has been unknown to any other people ancient or modern." [4]

Colleges have for two hundred years been important in American life in a way that is not identical with respect for learning in other cultures. The colleges have not always been good, but they have always been loved. And the financial support from millions of people has continued to verify the judgment of our second President. One measure of the greatness of the love of colleges is the extreme difficulty which we encounter when we try to eliminate one of them. Many have existed on a marginal economic basis for decades, only because some loyal people can always be found to balance the budget and to pay the debts, while professors work for almost nothing in order to keep the institutions alive. All this is part of the American story and it is a part worth cherishing.

In its most characteristic form, during most of our history, the American college has been neither governmental nor private. Though we have many states and municipal institutions, supported by general taxation, these do not represent our major tradition and have not, until recently, served the majority of the students. Even at this day the characteristic institution owes its origin to religious vitality and receives no money from tax funds, but it would be a complete misnomer to refer to such an institution as "private." It is not private because it does not exist for the profit of its owners; it does not limit itself to one denomination or party; and it accepts a high degree of responsibility for the cultivation of public taste and the encouragement of public service. The American college is, in fact, a public institution in the same sense that the English "public schools" are public; both are designed to serve the entire nation. This point was made so often and so well by Woodrow Wilson that it has come to be associated with his name. In his inaugural address as president of Princeton, he de-

[4] *The Political Writings Of John Adams* (New York: The Liberal Arts Press), pp. 11, 12.

nied the private character of his institution, even though it was not
tax-supported. "The service of institutions of learning," he said,
"is not private but public. It is plain what the nation needs as its
affairs grow more and more complex and its interests begin to
touch the ends of the earth. It needs efficient and enlightened
men." [5] There are many ways of differentiating between colleges,
but the distinction between the public and the private is perhaps
the least valuable.

In terms of contribution to the public good, the independent
institutions exhibit a high level of competence. Many readers
were surprised, in examining the findings of the ambitious study
made by Professors Robert H. Knapp and H. B. Goodrich of
Wesleyan University, to learn that of the colleges which have, per
capita, made the greatest contributions in science, thirty-nine out
of the top fifty institutions were those with independent boards
and support, usually comparatively small, and with a Christian
emphasis. Excellence was shown to have emerged in unsuspected
ways.

A striking difference between the independent college and its
tax-supported counterparts is that the former can be more truly
national in character. The better independent colleges gain enormously from the fact that they draw their students from all parts
of the nation. This is what the state university cannot normally do,
while the municipal college does it practically not at all. When
James Bryant Conant was president of Harvard, he pointed out, in
a public address at Bryn Mawr, that the independent colleges have
"the opportunity of being national institutions in a sense which is
all but impossible for the publicly supported colleges dependent
on local taxes, the chief concern of which is quite rightly with the
boys and girls of the city or state in which they are located."

A strange feature of our present academic situation is the fact

[5] Woodrow Wilson, "Princeton for the Nation's Service," *The Public
Papers Of Woodrow Wilson* (New York, Harper & Brothers, 1925), Vol. I,
p. 443.

that we are slightly ashamed of the college, and consequently apologetic. Sometimes we are apologetic about the college because it is different from its European counterpart.[6] On other occasions we seem to think a college is less valuable than a university because a university is bigger. A good many of our citizens would define a university as a large and prosperous college and a college as a second-rate university. But the only justification of such a judgment would be the conclusion, which is by no means self-evident, that bigness and excellence are somehow synonymous. A mountain is far superior in size to a diamond, but it may not be size that really counts. Indeed, as we become more critical of our assumptions, we realize that there can be genuine merit in smallness. If this is true, the right answer to the enormous demands involved in the increase in population is not to destroy our small colleges by making them big, but rather the decision to start new ones. This is the plan we shall follow if we come to believe, as many are now doing, that the idea of the small college, far from being a second-rate conception, really provides us with our best chance for greatness.

One of the reasons why the small college represents our best ideal is that it can produce a higher degree of unity than can any alternative academic organization with which we are acquainted. The modern university, part college, part graduate school, part professional school, has many advantages, but unity of aim is not one of them.

The old university had two typical characteristics both of which were expressed in its name. *Universitas* may mean: *universitas lit-*

---

[6] As early as 1852, President Henry P. Tappan of the University of Michigan proposed that the college idea be abandoned and that the German conception of the university be adopted in its place. In 1894 Woodrow Wilson mentioned this general proposal, saying, "We have been so often bidden by young and old alike, to make our university in structure like that of Germany." Wilson rejected the idea with the remark, "There is a very heavy duty on imported ideals." These words may apply to the contemporary temptation to follow the Russian pattern.

terarum and thus stand for the unity of the sciences in one integrated conception of the world. Or it may mean: *universitas magistrorum et scholarium* (this is the original meaning) and thus stand for an independent community held together by the ideal of common search for truth. But the modern university is neither.[7]

Whereas unity of aim and conviction seems virtually impossible of attainment in a contemporary university, it is still possible in a small college. Johns Hopkins University undoubtedly had genuine unity in the nineteenth century, but in those days the institution was not really large. We have a revealing insight into the early success of this noble institution in the words of Professor Rendel Harris, uttered just before he died. Looking back to the great sense of academic community of fifty years earlier, and being asked to explain it, he said, in 1939, "It was very simple; we all attended each other's lectures." Then he went on to point out how vividly it raised a man's sights to have scholars like Professor Gildersleeve or Dr. Osler or President Gilman as members of his audience. It is no wonder that the institution exhibited such intellectual vitality. The best minds were continually stimulating one another, instead of working always in departmental isolation. It is one of the great merits of a modern college that, in it, such a pattern is not intrinsically impossible even today. To our shame the embodiment of this ideal is not always attempted and, in some places, it is not even recognized as an ideal, but the exciting fact is that, in a small college with really high standards, it is still possible.

The word university, implying unity, is a good name, and the word college, implying community, is also a good name, but the latter has more chance of fidelity to its meaning than has the former. Not all colleges are places of a real sharing of life, in which each person is an individual instead of a number, and in which the worth of each individual is more than a pious American expression, but there are some colleges in which the achievement of this ideal is seriously attempted. It is still the standard experience for

[7] W. A. Visser 't Hooft, *None Other Gods* (New York: Harper & Brothers, 1937), p. 126.

the professor and his students to be genuine friends, not ashamed to be seen together, for most teaching is such that there is a truly personal relationship between teacher and taught. There is, on the other hand, a chance that the young person going to a college will be treated impersonally, but fortunately the chance is still slight.

The college exists in order to provide a situation of maximum rapid growth in the whole life of persons. It is a contrived means of bringing to bear maximum beneficent influence, in the hope of producing maximum progress in the lives of the individuals concerned. This is why the college is concerned with more than learning, in the narrow sense. Membership in a college involves far more than attendance at classes, and this is as it should be. Ideally, the members of a college, both teachers and taught, *work* together, *think* together, *play* together, and *pray* together. We must not allow any of these to act as substitutes for the others. We must not let our praying remain separate from our thinking or allow our playing to become wholly dissociated from our working. It is wholeness of life that we consciously and deliberately seek.

What the college hopes to produce in those under its care is not merely a knowledge of facts, which may be evanescent, or even illusory, but the ability to *judge*. The aim is the kind of mind that can judge which ones, among apparent facts, are really facts, and that, moreover, can do this in a great variety of fields. Especially we hope to develop acute and accurate judgment of men and movements and faiths. The end of education, said William James, is "knowing a good man when you see him." [8] In an equally memorable phrase a contemporary writer has said, "The most important science of all is the science of choice." [9] Because

8 William James, *Memories and Studies*, p. 309.
9 Tunis Romein, *Education and Responsibility* (Lexington: University of Kentucky Press, 1955), p. 61. See also Freya Stark in *The Lycian Shore*: "To produce the lifelong stimulus of choice in both thought and action should be the aim of all education."

man is free, in the sense that his actions are not wholly determined by forces outside his own mind and character, nothing is more important than the development of character in such a way that better and better choices are made. This cannot be accomplished in any easy or simple way. That is why the educational process is inevitably a long one, and a difficult one, if it is to be worth anything.

Because education is today big business, enjoying a boom, it is easy to lose sight of fundamental goals. It is easy to concentrate upon the construction of buildings and efficiency of administration without serious searching for the purpose, apart from which these are as nothing. Because attendance at college is fashionable today, thousands now enroll without any burning desire to learn and without any clear understanding of why they are in college at all. Students assemble in huge classes and walk from building to building, carrying heavy textbooks which serve effectively to keep them from better and greater reading. Often the whole undertaking seems more like that of a factory than anything else. It is booming, but to what end? Is it developing judgment in regard to literature or art or conduct? Is it producing creativity in science such that new discoveries will be made? Is it encouraging new imagination concerning the ways in which men can live together in real peace? Do people come out of this community more compassionate and more unified in their lives than they were when they entered? Do they emerge with the desire to go on learning and reading and exploring as long as they live? These are embarrassing questions, but they are the questions which we cannot afford not to ask. The right questions may be more important than anything else.

II

The Concept of a Christian College

"Unite the pair so long disjoin'd,
Knowledge and vital piety."
CHARLES WESLEY

THE Christian faith has affected the American pattern of existence
at many points, but at no point more vividly than in its academic
pattern. This is often poorly understood in other countries, the
false assumption being that a Christian college is devoted either
to religious studies or to denominational instruction of its members. In actual practice, however, practically no American college
follows such a plan. Each is devoted, instead, to many studies and
to many types of students, the uniqueness, if any, arising wholly
from the character of the fundamental commitment which per-
vades the entire enterprise. Since education and religion provide
us with the most enduring societies of human history, it did not
seem strange to our ancestors that the two should be combined
in one continuous effort. The combination of the love of God
and the love of learning was one which commended itself to the
early colonists because it seemed eminently reasonable. What
seemed equally reasonable was that colleges representing this fertile cross should start other colleges of a similar nature. Sixteen
of these, spread across the nation, were thus the offspring of Yale,
among them Western Reserve, Beloit, and Grinnell. Even a num-

ber of the state universities were built on Christian foundations. No scholar, of any nationality, can hope to understand American culture if he does not study carefully the immense impact of the Christian college upon the total American life.

With the growth of the country and the introduction of state universities, as well as the introduction of purely secular conceptions of education, it was natural that the relative unity of the early pattern would, in time, be broken. A number of the colleges founded by Christian conviction and sacrifice began to make conscious efforts to dissociate themselves from their roots, seeking to become ordinary secular institutions, though with no governmental connection either state or local. Others, desiring to throw off sectarian shackles which were in some cases hindrances to educational progress, succeeded, without an open break, in becoming as independent of church as of state. There was a widespread tendency, especially in the early decades of the present century, to be apologetic about the Christian basis of colleges and to play it down accordingly. Thus arose the odd nomenclature by which many colleges referred to themselves as "church-related." The term was, of course, intentionally ambiguous. Relationship, everyone knows, can be either distant or close. It may mean a great deal or it may mean practically nothing, and the simple truth is that the latter is what was often intended by "church-related."

In many instances the bond between the church and the college was broken concurrently by both members of the partnership. Not only was the college a little ashamed of its connection with the church; the church, often because of theological narrowness, frequently criticized the college it had helped to nourish and sometimes tacitly renounced it. Often the money contributed by the church to the college which it had founded and supposedly owned was only a small fraction of the total benefactions.

This growing separation between the colleges and their founding bodies was tragic. It was bad for the colleges, which became thereby increasingly rootless, and it was bad for the churches, which lost, in the divorce, the benefit of the sharp self-criticism which comes from disciplined intelligence. As the college came to adopt the liberal arts principle and nothing else, being dissociated in practice if not in name from its Christian basis, it really had no principle of organization except mere curiosity and loyalty to an abstract truth which nobody ever possesses. The church, on its side, fell into decay because it was increasingly out of touch with the world of science.

One of the most remarkable of the changes which have occurred in our century, and particularly about the middle of the century, has been a sharp reversal of this process of increasing divorce. Within a few years strong voices were raised in all parts of the country, and in all of the major churches, pointing to the necessity of a new start. The separation of the college from its religious roots began to be recognized, not as a liberation, but as an incalculable loss. Many saw the point of Thoreau's rejoinder to Emerson, when Emerson remarked that Harvard College then taught all the branches of learning. "Yes," said Thoreau, "all the branches, but none of the roots."

One vivid evidence of the new mood was the appearance of *The Mind's Adventure* by Howard Lowry, president of the College of Wooster. President Lowry, himself an eminent scholar, is also a committed Christian who has had the courage to declare himself in favor of the attempt to produce and maintain a Christian college. In his book there was notable absence of the apologetic mood, and of the familiar words about spiritual values in general. "The Christian college," he wrote, "will be, therefore, a community existing around a group of learners, both teachers and students, who confess Jesus Christ as their Savior and Lord. They are engaged in a serious search for the knowledge of God and His universe and His demands upon human life." [1]

Insofar as we care about our total culture we are bound to

[1] Howard Lowry, *The Mind's Adventure* (Philadelphia: The Westminster Press, 1950), pp. 102, 103.

think carefully concerning the right use of the institutions which constitute so great a part of America's cultural heritage. What are we to do with the Christian college? Three possibilities are bound to occur. The first is to accept the secularizing process and allow the colleges to become institutions of higher learning with little or no reference to the faith which spawned them. Since this has already occurred so widely, it might seem to be the path of wisdom to accept the inevitable and to rejoice in it. The words of the college seal may thereby become meaningless, while the chapel may become an anachronism, when the real temple is the main Technology Building, but human progress is inevitably ruthless. The march of civilization must not be resisted.

The second possibility is to turn the Christian college into an institution which is primarily a training school for church workers. It would, in that event, recover unity of aims, though at a terrible price. The price would be the essential abdication from the task of helping to form contemporary mentality in its many aspects, including the scientific, the literary, and the political. The first of these two proposals is unacceptable because it produces institutions which are both colorless and rudderless, while the second is unacceptable because it involves a retreat from the world. Real religion, said William Penn, does not take men out of the world but puts them into it, in the hope of bettering it.

The third solution, and the one to which so many vigorous minds are now giving their best thought, is that of maintaining the Christian college as one which seeks to demonstrate excellence in the sciences and in other major studies, striving to influence positively the course of contemporary civilization, not in separation from its religious roots but in an ever closer connection with them. Many now believe this to be our highest ideal, something far superior to an institution which is so secular that it has no positive unifying philosophy and equally superior to one which serves only the purposes of a religious group, without adequate reference to the needs of the world. This third possibility has reappeared in our time as a brilliant hope. It is the conception which inspired President Lowry's excellent book as well as the Quadrennial Convocations of Christian Colleges in 1954 and in 1958, and a host of intellectually exciting conferences in all parts of the nation.[2] The remainder of this chapter will be devoted to an attempt to state clearly the nature of this third possibility. The thesis is that a college so constituted represents, not some compromise or second best, but the actual best that we know. If fully understood, and truly embodied, the idea of the Christian college is better than any alternative of which we are able to conceive.

Since the central task of a college is its intellectual task, that is a good place at which to begin. Other things being equal, the Christian scholar is likely to be a better scholar because of the nature of his motivation. The eminence of avowedly Christian colleges in the natural sciences is surely no accident. Every good investigator wants to learn the truth, if he can, but the committed Christian has an added motive in that his intellectual task is a sacred task because it is God's truth that he is trying to learn. For the devout man, dishonesty in research or in reporting the results of research is worse than bad science; it is also blasphemy. The Christian faith, when it understands itself, is the sworn enemy of all intellectual dishonesty and shoddiness. That is one of the reasons why, no matter how bad the church becomes through human arrogance, the strongest critics are always those who are on the inside. All of the Christian revolutions have come from within. Luther, we must never forget, was a monk.

The work of the scientist takes on new vigor if he is a believer in the Living God, for he then realizes that his best efforts are efforts to think God's thoughts after him. The scholar is not really *inventing*; he is only *discovering*, and the realization of this fact

[2] The second Quadrennial Convocation of Christian Colleges, held in 1958, dealt more strictly with the theological basis of Christian education. Both gatherings have been fully reported in print.

keeps him intellectually humble. The laboratory worker is using all of his equipment to ask God a question. There are good scientists who are not avowed Christians, but much of their motivation is really a vestige of a world view which they have supposedly rejected. Whether they know it or not, they are living in the afterglow of a faith which makes shoddy research a sin and not merely bad form. Though mere curiosity is a weak motive, the effort to understand God's laws is an extremely powerful motive. This motive will remain for a while after the decline of the faith which inspires it, but it will not remain forever unless it is consciously and deliberately renewed. The first reason, then, for the superiority of the Christian college is that the religious scholar has more reason to be careful of his evidence than has the nonreligious scholar, in that he is handling what is intrinsically sacred. There is some justification for A. E. Housman's famous remark that "the love of truth is the faintest of human passions," but the situation is altered if what we face is God's truth.

Few intellectual changes of our time have been more striking than that in regard to objectivity. In the recent past, the view was widely held in academic circles that a man had to be neutral in his convictions in order to be objective and trustworthy. The fact that a man was a convinced and committed Christian, in the sense mentioned above, was held, in some circles, to be a disqualification for a teacher, even in religious subjects. Thus it was supposed that the atheist scholar would be better able to teach the history of religion because he would not take sides in the controversies and could look at all issues with Olympian detachment. The curious illogicality of this position was revealed by the fact that the same principle was not applied elsewhere. A man was not equally disqualified to teach art because of his commitment to art and nobody was rash enough to suppose that commitment to the aims and methods of science constituted a disqualification for scientific teachers or researchers. Religion was put in a special class as a result of a nineteenth-century cast of mind which was much engrossed with the idea of a perennial warfare between science and religion, strangely blind to the fact that so much of the best science had already been nourished in religiously grounded colleges. The assumption was, and sometimes still is, in the words of Bishop Pike, "that a 'believer' or 'practitioner' will be prejudiced and biased, but that one who rejects 'the supernatural' will be neutral and 'scientific,' as are presumably the members of other departments." Pike's answer to this position is convincing.

Actually nobody is objective. Everybody has a perspective, a world-view. And one's world-view is taken on faith, it is not proven. It is where one starts one's proving or testing. If a professor has a Biblical world-view he has it on faith; if one has the secularist world-view it is because he has chosen to narrow his frame of reference to what he calls "natural," or perhaps even to material phenomena. Data that overflow this confined frame he seeks to explain in terms of reality within the frame, whereas one with a roomier world-view is not under this necessity. A man is what he is: his own beliefs color his interpretation, his very selection of materials. This is not to say that a secularist should not teach Religion (or any other subject). It is merely to point out that neutrality toward religion has not been achieved by this solution.[3]

The claim that scholars can be impartial or neutral in anything of human importance is now an outmoded idea. Man finds himself inevitably in the value-centric predicament, because the very rejection of value judgments is itself a value judgment. The position of the thinker who is wholly clear of all assumptions is one which is neither desirable nor possible. What is important, in intellectual honesty, is that basic assumptions or perspectives should be understood, admitted, and cogently defended.

[3] James A. Pike, "Religion in Higher Education and the Problem of Pluralism," *Christianity and Crisis*, Vol. X, No. 23, p. 179. Bishop Pike's position receives strong support in the thinking of Dr. George A. Buttrick of Harvard University, especially in his highly quotable sentence, "One of the sorriest assumptions of secular education is that it makes no assumptions." See his *Christ and Man's Dilemma* (Nashville: Abingdon-Cokesbury Press, 1946), p. 138.

The change which has come is largely the result of strong blows which have been dealt the neutral assumption by a number of first-rate thinkers, including Paul Tillich and Reinhold Niebuhr. To be detached from that of which the very essence is involvement is, as Tillich has pointed out, a manifest absurdity. The claim to objectivity, in the sense of having no fixed starting point and consequently no position of reference, is an empty claim in any field of thought. The testimony of the late Carl Becker, one of the most eminent of secular historians, is sharp and clear on this point, especially in the following sentence: "Complete detachment would produce few histories, and none worth while; for the really detached mind is a dead mind, lying among the facts of history like unmagnetized steel among iron-filings, no synthesis ever resulting, in one case or the other, to the end of time." [4]

Among those who have come out clearly for the idea that a college, as well as its individual professors, has an obligation to make its point of view known is the president of Swarthmore College, who has spoken as follows:

If religious presuppositions are a shaping influence in our interpretation, we should articulate these presuppositions. Because, when in the name of science, or neutrality, or objectivity, we refuse to let it be known what values we value, students will graduate from school with the feeling that values don't count for much at all, with the result that they'll balk at religious, or moral, or ethical, or political commitment, or stake everything on getting ahead in this world, which will always be viewed in a materialistic way, or they will confuse opinion surveys and statistics, like Kinsey's, with standards. [5]

Students in a college, who are inevitably under the influence of the minds of professors, have a right to know what the positions

---

[4] Carl L. Becker, *Detachment and the Writing of History* (Ithaca, N.Y.: Cornell University Press, 1958), p. 24.

[5] Courtney C. Smith, "Contributions of Quakerism to Education," *The Westonian*, Vol. LXII, No. 3, p. 6.

are which professors take on major issues, including the basic pre-suppositions with which they begin. The professor who does not have the courage to state his own position, both unapologetically and humbly, is not likely to win the enduring respect of those who are under his care. This is a point on which the careful report called "Amherst Tomorrow" is especially clear.

There has been a tendency in recent years to insist on what is mistakenly called "academic objectivity" in teaching, that is, to insist that a teacher should refrain from expressing any opinion on controversial issues or indicating what he sincerely believes on questions of vital human import. We believe this position to be thoroughly mistaken.

In the first place, no teacher worthy of the name can avoid having convictions on vital issues, and no teacher can actually succeed in hiding these convictions from his students no matter how hard he may try to do so. Secondly, the student is much less likely to be victimized by the professor's beliefs if they are stated openly and if the student is told, as he should be, that he is under obligation to accept them or reject them only on his own responsibility and at his own peril. . . . Thirdly, we believe that students should be made to realize that responsible men do make up their minds, however tentatively, on questions of importance and that men are under moral obligation to do so.[6]

The important point to elucidate is that the two familiar alternatives of complete detachment, on the one hand, and the spirit of propaganda, on the other, do not exhaust the logical possibilities. The third possibility is that mood in which each professor, while making his own position clear, seeks to be fair to all competing positions, to present the problems as vigorously as he presents the answers, and to go out of his way to point out the difficulties inherent in the position he presumably adopts.[7]

[6] "Amherst Tomorrow, A Report of the Alumni Committee on Post War Amherst College," *Amherst Alumni Council News*, Vol. XVIII, No. 3, pp. 95, 96.

[7] Unamuno was advocating this third possibility when he admonished intellectuals to stop treating ideas like concubines. They should, he said, have the courage to marry some great idea and raise children.

Clarity on the matter of academic detachment is a necessary preliminary to the fuller explication of what a Christian college is. A Christian college is one in which the Christian perspective is accepted openly, avowedly, and unapologetically. Those who are concerned with the encouragement of the Christian college are wholly willing for other institutions to start from other premises, but they say clearly that this is *theirs*. A thorough understanding of this starting point helps to determine the nature of the curriculum, the selection of professors, and the entire spirit of the academic community. The acceptance of a firm starting point of Christian conviction about nature, about man, and about God is far more important than some official connection with a church. Some of the colleges with church connections make no serious effort to start from an avowed Christian perspective in all phases of college life, while other colleges, which are not church-connected, make their Christian philosophy explicit. There are inevitable differences in the details of the understanding of the Christian position, but the central starting point is reasonably definite. *It is the conviction that both man and the world of nature are best understood as creatures of the Divine Mind who is accurately revealed in Jesus Christ.*

It is a complete misunderstanding of the academic situation to suppose that the Christian emphasis can be made sufficiently by auxiliary enterprises, with little or no consideration of the central educational task. We can be grateful for the discussions which go on in the Wesley Foundation or the Newman Club or the Y.M.C.A., but these will never suffice if the positions represented in these auxiliary organizations are daily undermined by the influence of leading instructors or by the college policy. The sad truth is that much of what the denominational counselors do seems far removed from the central intellectual questions which the college must encourage students to ask and to try to answer if it is to be worthy of its major vocation. The following observations of a British visitor to America may seem harsh, but they provide a wholesome warning:

America has more full-time students' chaplains, whether appointed by the Y.M.C.A. or the churches, in universities of all kinds than any other country in the world. Yet, while a surprising number of these gentlemen show, to the astonished admiration of European visitors, a virtuosity in devising spontaneous entertainments equal to that of the great Danny Kaye himself, their intellectual responsibilities appear to sit very lightly upon their shoulders. With a few shining exceptions their purpose in the university appears to be to run a bigger and better young people's group than in the church back home.[8]

The Christian character of a college is attested, not by what goes on at the fringes and not even by the existence of scholarly courses in Biblical studies or the history of religion. The Christian character is attested by the mood and conviction of the major teaching of the institution. The Christian commitment of the men who teach sociology and philosophy and biology may be far more a revelation of the Christian character of a college than is the commitment of the man who teaches New Testament, for this may be assumed. In the subjects mentioned, as well as many others, we must seek to enlist able scholarship, but the truth is that, in every one of them, the professor's presuppositions will show through his treatment of his theme. There is reason to believe that a man is a better psychologist if he is also a committed Christian. This is not because piety can ever dispense with technique, nor character substitute for scholarship, but because the Christian operates from a broader base than can those who are limited by adherence to contemporary and passing secular fashions. The Christian psychologist will learn from Freud, but he will also learn from Augustine and his study of the Bishop of Hippo will enable him to see some of the self-contradictions which are to be found in the work of the doctor of Vienna.

The acceptance of a point of reference will help the Christian college in its selection of the persons who are to be given the high privilege and responsibility of influencing the minds and

[8] Daniel Jenkins, "The Crisis in the University," *Christianity and Crisis*, Vol. IX, p. 166.

thereby the lives of the students. When the Christian standpoint is taken seriously, it becomes a criterion of selection. The atheist who seeks to be popular and to win a reputation for boldness by his efforts to unsettle the students in their religious faith will not be welcomed. There may be a place for him, but the Christian college is not that place. The college can get along without the assistance of those who are flippant or who sit in the seat of the scornful. There are certain assumptions that a man cannot make and, at the same time, be an integral part of a Christian college. He cannot, for example, assume, as many now do, that human life is adequately explained by mechanism, that mind and brain are identical conceptions, or that human behavior is merely a matter of stimulus and response. A man is out of place in a Christian college if he denies the reality of human freedom and the responsibility which is meaningless apart from this freedom.

A reasonable question is how much variety a college can include and still maintain its character or make its rightful impact on society. It is fashionable to say that every viewpoint should be represented, but this, as we analyze it, is nonsense. There are not enough positions, even in a great university, for every possible viewpoint to be represented and certainly there are not enough in a small college. Furthermore, it is not necessary for viewpoints to be *represented* in order for them to be presented. Because a good Christian scholar can present dialectical materialism with real fairness, at the same time expressing his own criticism, it is not necessary to employ an avowed Communist on the faculty.

A certain unity is necessary if intellectual confusion and waste of effort are to be avoided. Let us say that two men are to handle the department of philosophy. Does intellectual integrity demand that one of these be a theist and the other an atheist? Of course not. The result of such conflict might mean that each would succeed only in canceling the influence of the other, with little profit to the student community. Obviously we do not want to have complete uniformity, and we are not likely to get it if we try, but much of the glory of the college lies in the fact that it is a manageable society in which a general unity of tone is possible, so that the impact made on minds is something more than confusion. It is partly because the large university cannot achieve this that Sir Walter Moberly and others have contended that the Christian university is an impossibility. The Christian college is a possibility and its possibility stems from the fact that it can achieve a unity of impact which is based upon thoughtful selection.

It is not required that every professor in a Christian college be a Christian of a particular type or even a Christian at all, but it is required that each one be understanding of Christian thought and reverent in the face of the great historic convictions. This leaves a place for a thoughtful Jew and it can even leave a place for the humble atheist, providing he has faced the issues squarely and, because of the genuine difficulties of theistic faith, feels, in loyalty to truth as he sees it, that he cannot affirm the theistic conclusion. He would be badly out of place, however, if he felt condescension toward theology. You cannot rightly look down on theology unless you have studied it sufficiently to transcend it. Pascal could afford to minimize philosophy only because he was a great philosopher. The college certainly cannot profit by the assistance of those who are contemptuous of that which they do not know. The college can survive and perform its vocation in the intellectual world with some deviation, but it cannot do so unless there is at the center a strong band, in both the sciences and other studies, that sees science as one of the noblest praises of God because it is the understanding of what God has made. The chief defense of this approach is that it breeds a deep intellectual humility which in turn produces better science.

Part of the value of Christian professors depends upon what they do while they are engaged in formal instruction and part of it depends upon what they do outside the classroom. One mark of a scholar who takes his Christian conviction seriously is that he is likely to share reverently with his colleagues and students in public worship. The late Archbishop Temple, who had much experience of colleges, felt so strongly about this that he maintained that a resident Fellow of a college who, being a professed Christian, is not frequent and regular in attendance at the daily service in his College Chapel is a fraudulent trustee for the treasure committed to him in his own faith. The professor of biology, deeply respected by students for his work in the laboratory, may accomplish far more than he realizes by the apparently simple act of kneeling in prayer. Students may remember this act long after they have forgotten some of his specific teachings. The Christian college is, by its nature, a fellowship of both prayer and study, a fellowship which requires demonstration even more than explanation.[9]

We must never forget that scholars are also men. They are men with the same needs and temptations that come to others. Those who teach also need a Teacher and, what is more, they need a Savior, exactly as unlearned men and women do. "Jesus Christ," warns Étienne Gilson, the famous French philosopher, "did not come to save men by science or philosophy. He came to save all men; even scientists and philosophers. Science and philosophy are not necessary to salvation; they themselves need salvation." A person who feels that he is self-sufficient, or that his intellectual discipline is self-sufficient, is not likely to feel at home in a truly Christian college.

If a Christian college could be achieved by the expedient of offering courses in religion, it would be a simple matter and most colleges would qualify. Nearly all of the tax-supported, as

[9] Long after he had ceased to be a professor at Harvard, George Herbert Palmer made his way, almost every morning, to share in daily prayers at Appleton Chapel. He thereby influenced generations of students whose names he never knew. In like manner President Pusey has, in more recent years, accomplished much by his regular reading of the lesson in the Sunday chapel service.

well as the independent, institutions offer courses in religion
and many announce religious departments. But the mere appearance of a religious course in a catalogue may mean little and
frequently it does. It means little when these courses are handled
in a marginal fashion, with no incentive to elect them and with
no real emphasis *upon* them. Christianity as an elective, similar
to archaeology, misses entirely the conception of the Christian
faith as the dynamic needed for both the criticism and the achievement of the goals of civilization. If Christianity is an adornment,
it is hardly worth the trouble, but it is not intended to be an adornment.

The Christian college is marked not by the mere offer of religious studies, but by giving them centrality and consequent
emphasis.[10] The student will come to believe that such studies
are taken seriously if they are so placed in the total system of
offerings that most students actually encounter them. Far from
being a marginal elective, the study of the Biblical heritage and
of the Christian faith is obviously more relevant today than it
has been for years. This is because the people of the West, aware
at last that competitive coexistence is the enduring contemporary
fact, are in great danger of copying the Russians in their effort to
surpass their brilliant competitors. This is what we do when we
try to overcome one kind of secularism by adopting another.
Our danger is that we will join the progress of dialectical materialism, not by conscious conversion to its philosophy, but by a
failure to be sufficiently self-critical to recognize and maintain the
elements of strength in our own position. The Christian college
must be rethought and rebuilt, not because we propose to main-

10 In actuality, theology cannot be avoided. If it is not taught in one way
it will be taught in another, because it deals with questions which students
ask. Newman clarified this point in the following way: "And lastly . . . suppos-
ing Theology be not taught, its province will not simply be neglected, but will
be actually usurped by other sciences, which will teach, without warrant, conclusions of their own in a subject matter which needs its own proper principles for its due formation and disposition." *The Idea of a University* (London: Longmans, Green & Company, 1929), p. 98.

tain, sentimentally, an outgrown system of life and thought, but because the principles which such a college embodies are peculiarly relevant to the complex needs of our generation.

What we need is a recovery of essential human dignity, and this is more likely to come through a theocentric humanism than it is through one which is merely anthropocentric. Man, as a finite creature, here for a little while before the blow falls, is not impressive and certainly he is not always lovely. But man, of any color or nationality, who is made in the image of the Living God, the Creator and Sustainer of the universe, is something radically different. He is worthy of respect, not because of what he is, but of what he represents, and what, under God, he may become. A Christian philosophy has more chance of developing a reasonable theory of responsibility than has any of its competitors. Human dignity comes not from "man the measure," but from "God the Measure." In and of himself alone a man is a poor, weak thing at best; but as a child of God, as revealed in Christ, he, though erring and foolish, is a creature of infinite possibility and ultimate worth.

The idea of the Christian college will not achieve embodiment unless there are several people bound together for this specific end. The lone professor, however keenly he senses the importance of the idea, is almost sure to be defeated, and his individual crusade will die with him. It is different, however, if several join together, in order to strengthen each other and thus to make a joint impact. Twenty years ago, a number of thoughtful men began to propose seriously the formation of a Christian Professors' Movement, a movement which could operate in either avowedly Christian institutions or in wholly secular ones. One of the clearest voices in the beginning was that of Dr. Visser 't Hooft, when he said, "We need something like special congregations of Christians in each of the main intellectual vocations. We need not only a Student Christian Movement which makes study a main part of its program, but also fellowship of Christian doctors and scientists and politicians. And we need very specially a Christian Professors' Movement." [11]

The notion of a guild of Christian professors has taken hold in many parts of the United States and bids fair to become an important feature in our future academic development. As early as 1939, the "Guild of Scholars" was organized by members of the Protestant Episcopal Church, most of whom were practicing teachers in colleges and universities. Their announced purpose was "to preserve and clarify the profile of historic Christianity in the thinking and reading and teaching of its members," and "to promote this clarification on our college and university campuses." The members of this Guild may teach any subject in any department, but they are determined to try to perform their academic duties, whatever they are, in the light of the Christian message. A great impetus has been given to this general movement by a number of national foundations, the most far-reaching being the work of the Danforth Foundation of St. Louis. The main aspects of this movement are carefully presented in a booklet, *The Faculty Christian Fellowship*, produced by J. Edward Dirks, editor of *The Christian Scholar*.[12]

It is becoming increasingly clear that if we are to have Christian colleges, the Christian faith must be applied to the total institutions. It is not enough to have a Student Christian Movement or a Professors' Christian Movement. The college does not automatically become Christian by establishing a religious course or by building a chapel in a central location, though both of these may be important. The entire atmosphere must be charged by Christian concern which, when it is real, produces both more integrity of scholarship and a deeper sense of responsibility. The achievement of this total atmosphere is not an easy task, but sometimes it is approximated and, when it is, it is self-validating.

[11] Visser 't Hooft, *None Other Gods*, p. 138.
[12] Available at the Commission on Christian Higher Education, National Council of the Churches of Christ in the U.S.A., 257 Fourth Ave., New York, N.Y.

Christian emphasis, in order to be real, must be something integral rather than something added. It must be at the center, rather
than the periphery. In our time, no word on this subject has been
wiser than that of William Clark when he said, "The Christian
college does not *have* a religious program; it *is* a religious program."

III

The Teacher

"Make sure of your teacher and forget about everything else."
CHARLES MALIK

IF there is any one conclusion on which there is conspicuous agreement in our current philosophy of education it concerns the supreme importance of the good teacher. It is easy to envisage a good college with poor buildings, but it is not possible to envisage a good college with poor teachers. Brilliant and stimulating teaching could go on in temporary barracks without any significant loss to the academic enterprise, but shoddy teaching means failure, even if it is conducted in palaces. We are wise to pay serious attention to the eloquent words of Charles Malik, who is at once a philosopher and a statesman, being a better statesman because he is also a philosopher.

The good teacher is the supreme actual instance of the conception of man and the universe on which liberal education is predicated. He has developed his reason, consequently he knows, he is in touch with the truth, he rejoices in its vision, and he can, through his art, impart that vision to others. And this noblest of all arts is the patient and loving leading of the student to see what the teacher himself sees, and this through problems, questions, tasks, challenges, puzzlement, discussion—and all—and this is the crucial thing—in the certain presence of the perfected knowledge of the teacher himself. The

33

teacher is to the student what the end is to the process, what the agent is to the patient, what the perfected form is to the material out of which it arises, what attainment is to struggle, what the rest of knowledge is to the twilight of opinion, what the certainty of being is to the flux of becoming, in short, what actuality is to potentiality.[1]

Admittedly this is a high ideal, but in view of the needs of our civilization it is not too high. If any considerable number of college instructors begin to accept this ideal as their standard, their sights will be so raised that we shall see a new day in our total academic life. Our task is to recover the sense of glory which the art of teaching involves.

We are fortunate that in this task we have today some strong allies. Eminent among these is Gilbert Highet of Columbia, whose book *The Art of Teaching*, has been reprinted many times since its first appearance in 1950 and has been a source of vision to many teachers, both in school and college. "Teaching," he says in his Preface, "is not like inducing a chemical reaction: it is much more like painting a picture or making a piece of music, or on a lower level like planting a garden or writing a friendly letter. You must throw your heart into it, you must realize that it cannot all be done by formulas, or you will spoil your work, and your pupils, and yourself."

Insofar as we care about that precious inheritance, the college, we must care about the development of teaching, with an eye to its dangers and to its means of improvement, always in the hope that teaching may thereby become great. But, first of all, there is merit in pointing out the happiness of the teacher who has found his vocation and understands its glory. Perhaps the greatest element in this happiness is the sense of self-respect which teaching can engender. It is unfortunately true that a great many men seem destined, in our kind of society, to spend

[1] Charles Malik, "The Significance of Christian Liberal Arts for Our Times," in *Our Best Chance for Greatness* (Indianola, Iowa: Simpson College, 1954), p. 22.

their major energies in tasks which they would never willingly perform, apart from the necessity of earning bread for themselves and their families. Most of these tasks are honorable and can, by a rational process, be understood as valuable, in that they involve goods or services which human beings need or by which they profit. Thus it is possible to argue that the bond salesman and the advertiser, far from being parasites, are helping the whole task of production and distribution on which an industrial society inevitably depends.

Worthy as may be the effort of other men to justify their labor and hence their existence, the teacher does not need to engage in such an elaborate undertaking at all, because the dignity and worth of his labor are self-evident. The chief rewards of the teacher's life are intrinsic, not subsidiary. No defense is required of work in which we try to bring knowledge or vision to persons who, without such effort on the part of some deeply concerned teacher, might never possess these valuable assets. Millions must work every day at jobs which, in the nature of the case, require no real alertness, no significant decisions, and very little intelligence. The teacher, by contrast, is dealing continually with what is manifestly important. He is not using his wits to persuade his fellow men that one brand of whiskey is superior to others of its kind, when he knows that there is no appreciable difference between them. Instead, he is dealing with great themes and with malleable personalities, in which the fruits of his influence may be momentous for good or for ill. Millions of jobs are of such a nature that only the money makes them bearable, but teaching is not one of these.

The teacher is a person who illustrates, to a marked degree, Aristotle's famous point about happiness arising in the course of creation. To create anything may bring a certain joy, but creation in the realm of the personal is obviously higher in value than is creation in the realm of the merely material or mechanical. The teacher who understands his calling is made happy every day by the chance to participate, sometimes successfully and sometimes not, in the making of differences in human lives. The good teacher is usually a happy person, primarily because he is a maker, and men were made to make. This is the deep significance of the ancient Hebrew insight to the effect that man is made in the image of God. Men and women are made in God's image, not materially but functionally; they can share modestly in creation. No one understands this better than the teacher who loves his work.

Though real teaching requires a tremendous expenditure of energy and cannot be done well without a sense of tonus in the body as well as the mind, there is a wonderful way in which the teacher's energy is sustained in the midst of the task, providing he loves what he is doing. Professor Highet's reference to this, a reference obviously autobiographical, has struck a responsive note in others:

Such a man is borne upwards and swept onwards by energy which flows into him from outside, from the group of which he is the heart and the voice. The good teacher feels that same flow of energy, constantly supplied by the young. If he can canalize it, he will never be tired. At least, not while he is teaching.[2]

It is in the light of such magnificent rewards as those just mentioned that we must consider the question of the payment of teachers. Today there is a great public demand for more money with which to give larger teacher salaries. No doubt this is a valuable effort, but it is fundamentally erroneous insofar as it encourages people to believe that we can get better teachers by raising salaries. Not every problem can be solved by allotting dollars. Undoubtedly we seek a situation in which professors can pay their bills and educate their own children without undue strain or the constant search for new sources of revenue in order to balance the family budget, but good teaching cannot be bought.

[2] Gilbert Highet, *The Art of Teaching* (New York: Vintage Books, 1956), p. 27.

The best teachers have nearly always stayed at the job in spite of genteel poverty, because the task itself is intrinsically appealing. Adequate salaries are necessary, but they are not and can never be sufficient incentives. The crucial element in the process is commitment to a task which is inherently noble and ennobling. Unless a teacher grasps this, he is not likely to do a good job, even though he might be paid as much as an automotive engineer. Professors who are unhappy and who complain of their lot ought to find some other line of work, for the unhappy teacher will never be the good teacher.

Few in our time have been as fortunate as the late Bliss Perry in explaining the secret of great teaching, particularly in his auto-biographical book *And Gladly Teach*. The Chaucerian title itself carries the idea, but the entire book bears it out. What a fortunate life Professor Perry had as he taught at Williams and Princeton and Harvard, and edited the *Atlantic Monthly!* All of his mature life was carried on in an atmosphere of greatness and of participation in molding young minds. But always his supreme joy came in the performance of the work itself. Even after years of teaching, he knew better than to ride on the work of the past for a single day. If he was scheduled to teach the next morning, he would excuse himself from a party in progress and repair to his study because each performance had to be fresh. If it were not fresh, he felt, it would be second-rate, and he could never be satisfied to settle for that.[3]

The question is often asked whether a teacher's first responsi-bility is to know his subject or to know his students. This question is essentially unanswerable, being similar to the question of which sex is more necessary for procreation. The good teacher must know his subject and he must know his students and he must know both at once. The scholar's concern for the subject under inquiry

[3] See *And Gladly Teach* (Boston: Houghton Mifflin Company, 1935), p. 261. Perry's confession was, "I worry over a lecture for days and weeks beforehand, enjoy the actual hour of teaching enormously, and then suffer acute misery in reflecting how I might have bettered the instruction."

is more fruitful if always the needs of the students are in the back of his mind, and his personal interest in young people is more valuable if it involves some truth which he is burning to impart. Subject and person are as necessary to each other as are the two blades of a pair of scissors.

The good teacher's approach to his subject is rightly one of reverence. Almost always it is an old subject hammered out by the long dialogue of successive thinkers and generations of thinkers. Consequently he is humble as he contemplates its vastness and the price that has already been paid for its development. He is so conscious of standing on the shoulders of many that it would be sacrilege to misrepresent what has thereby been revealed. His knowing is, of course, subjective, but what he knows is not subjective at all, for the truth of a proposition antedates both its verification and the recognition of it. The more honest and really clear two scholars are, the closer will be their conclusions to one another, because both are dealing with the same objective reality. Their differences are merely a mark of the inadequacy of one or both of them. Lord Acton made this point vivid by his observation that a life of Luther written by a Roman Catholic historian would be essentially the same as a life written by a Protestant historian, providing both men were equally scholarly and therefore equally honest in thier judgments.

Mark Van Doren has made a similar point in his essay "The Responsibility of The Teacher," especially in his emphasis on the nonindividual character of a teacher's knowledge. The fact that a man is personal need not mean that he is queer or marked by idiosyncracies. "Good persons," says Van Doren, "know the same things, just as they resemble one another. The ultimate paradox is that the things one must learn for oneself are the things all serious persons must learn. There is only one world for the multitude of persons in it to recognize." [4] The teacher's purpose is to take students out of the partial worlds which are the product of

[4] In *The Mount Holyoke Alumnae Quarterly*, Winter 1958, pp. 146, 147.

their own misguided imaginations or their own partial and therefore distorted viewpoints, in order to introduce them to the "only
world that is or ever will be." No person, whether student or
teacher, ever glimpses this one true world in its entirety, but the
fact that we do not reach perfection is no good reason for failing to
try to remove those imperfections which are humanly removable.

Though the good teacher cannot know everything, even about
a small area of knowledge, he can be so filled with the glory of his
subject that the student who is reasonably open to such influences
may be deeply moved by his teacher's reverence for truth. Thus
the good teacher is not the kind of actor who draws attention to
himself and his own peculiarities, but one who is so in love with
his subject that he practically becomes anonymous in its presence.
The good teacher is humble, not in the sense that he depre-
ciates himself, but in the far more profound sense that he forgets
himself. Real humility is not thinking badly of oneself; real humility is not thinking of oneself at all. The first-class speaker is so
lost in his subject, and in the response of his hearers, that he never
stops to ask himself how he is progressing. This kind of self-forget-
fulness is something which the good student will always respect,
even though he may not analyze it consciously.

The supremacy of Shakespeare, Van Doren points out, is not
that "he saw what nobody ever saw before." This, in fact, he did
not do. Instead, "he saw what everyone has seen, but with a clarity,
an intensity, and finally a humility which makes his subject even
more interesting to us than he is." In like manner, we really know
comparatively little about the life and character and personality
of Plato, but, through him as the supremely gifted and disciplined
teacher, we know a great deal about his own teacher, as well as
about justice and knowledge and courage and the way in which
they are related to one another. The good teacher is like clear glass,
which functions best when it is not seen at all.

The methods of the good teacher are many and are best used in
conjunction. One method is the lecture, which has not been out-

moded by the invention of printing or of radio or television or by any other known device. In each college generation someone comes along to say that lecturing is no longer valuable, but his point is continually refuted by the experience of those few professors who know how to lecture, both artistically and effectively. Some truths are best expressed by the living voice of a good teacher, when his method of presentation compels greater attention than the printed page can normally command. The fact that there are a hundred students in the room, rather than ten, does not diminish the power of the good lecturer at all and may, in fact, enhance his power. There can be a sense of intellectual excitement with a considerable company, particularly if the lecture room is rightly arranged and just barely large enough to accommodate all of those present. Since nothing harms a lecturer more than empty seats, the mood is usually better if one or two extra chairs must be brought in.

Let no one suppose that the physical setting for good teaching is irrelevant. We can learn something, in this regard, from the determination of Sir Winston Churchill, when the House of Commons was rebuilt, that the hall should not be large enough to seat more than two-thirds of the members. He knew from long experience that a full house greatly lifts the general tone of debate and he knew, also, that he could not expect 100 per cent attendance. A small audience in a large room is dispiriting, but a full room is helpful.

Artistic lecturing is far from the stupid exercise in which a man pulls out a faded manuscript or even galley sheets and simply proceeds to read. This is poor, partly because it is too easy. The only successful alternative is that in which the lecturer has prepared himself so well that he speaks with flexibility, often without looking at notes at all. He knows where he is going, but he adjusts all of the intermediate steps to the needs of his hearers. He is always watching their eyes, and if it is evident from the way the students look that a point has not been made clear, he tries again in another way. There are many evils involved in the practice of reading a manuscript, but the worst of these is that attention to the text keeps the teacher from looking at his students when he needs to see them. Above all, the human contact must be maintained.

Students do not have much respect for a professor if he does not know where he is going. Confidence is built by the recognition that the lecturer has a plan for the entire course and that all of the major steps lead in the same direction. Usually it is helpful if a blackboard can be used to present the main outline of each lecture in such a manner that the students see exactly where they are in each part of the hour. Always the aim is clarity, for the professor is a failure when he is not lucid, whatever other virtues he may demonstrate.

Good lecturing is valuable in that it brings a sense of personal excitement to intellectual inquiry and exhibits dramatically the direct contact between minds which is central to the idea of a college. Such lecturing does not supplant either reading or discussion, but supplements and undergirds both. The good lecture is far more a beginning than an end. It succeeds insofar as it stirs up the discussion and the personal conversation between professor and students, or between student and student, which represent the real success of the academic undertaking. The lecture is usually a good one if, when it is over, several of those who have been present gather over the coffee cups to continue the same theme with prolonged and heated argument. It is because this outcome is so desirable that it is a mistake to have an academic day closely or tightly scheduled. Not all will use the free time well, but some will do so, and the fact that they do justifies the arrangement of free time. In the ordinary American college we tend to overschedule every day, so that students are always going to classes or listening to lectures until they are surfeited and do not have time to engage in the reflection or discussion without which even the best of lectures is incomplete. We should be wise to lecture less and lecture better. Most classes meet too often.

Great as is the skill required of the lucid lecturer, the skill of one who can guide a profitable dialogue is even greater. This necessitates the expenditure of enormous mental energy necessary to provide guidance, for the discussion is almost worthless if it is a mere wrangle with no direction. Expert guidance is difficult because it must be relatively inconspicuous. The teacher must guide without dominating; he must know how to bring the talk back to some fruitful line; he must repress the overvocal; he must pull out the timid. Here the Platonic dialogues provide our classic model, with the professor taking the part of Socrates. Consequently he will often encourage the students to ask questions of him, but his ideal will be to help them to answer their own questions and thus be participators in the intellectual quest rather than parasites.

There is a place for what is called recitation, but that place is seldom found in a college. To assign ten pages and then to quiz the students on them in the presence of fellow students is too elementary. The method of direct question to ascertain whether material has been understood may, however, be wholly appropriate in the tutorial hour when the professor is closeted with one student at a time. Then the element of embarrassment is largely eliminated, and the student may come to have such a wholesome sense of his own failure to comprehend that he is encouraged to do better.

There is no magic in discussion. It is often unsuccessful and is, indeed, almost sure to be so unless the conditions of success are carefully planned in advance. Often a serious barrier is the physical arrangement. Only a genius can conduct a fruitful discussion among people who are seated in straight rows, audience style. Many of the barriers are removed if all can sit around a table, preferably a large one. The fact that all involved, professor and students alike, have their feet under the same table is one of greater value than the inexperienced would suppose. Such an arrangement is increasingly used by those who care greatly about their teaching.

Sometimes discussion is a sheer waste of time, and it is nearly always so when it becomes an occasion in which the superficially bright student can shine without doing any preliminary work at all. The wise professor must understand this and see to it that such superficiality does not go unchallenged, or receive a disproportionate reward. Discussion can be valuable for clarification and for the sharpening of ideas, but it must never be accepted as a substitute for work. The give and take of dialogue is most valuable when it follows individual study and when it leads to further individual study. The best teachers do not content themselves with lecturing while they leave all conduct of discussion periods to lesser officers. It is good for the students to see the professor in more than one role, and to confront him directly.

In a good college ample physical arrangements will be made for private and uninterrupted conversation between professors and individual students. This is why Thomas Jefferson was insistent that professorial residences should be intermingled with student residences when he planned the arrangements at Charlottesville. The college is really becoming a college, in at least one sense, when, the professor and the student having met on the campus, the professor invites the student to his study to look at books and to continue the conversation in an unhurried way. Many, now in mature life, can trace the real moments of intellectual birth to such occasions. Perhaps, when money is scarce, there should be more spent on the construction of studies and less on classrooms. We must create a tradition in which experiences of student-teacher conversation are expected as normal elements of college life. It is, however, only honest to report that there are colleges in which occasions of this kind are so rare as to be practically unknown. Students are afraid of friendliness with professors for fear of being tagged by their fellow students as seekers of special privilege. A fear as deep-seated as this will not be eliminated with ease, but those who care about the college will never rest until this pattern of expectation is radically changed. One way to change it is to point out continually that the fear in question is a mark of adolescence, not a mark of maturity. The mature student will always try to gain the most that he can from his contact with his teacher and not care in the least what his fellow students think about the matter.

The time may come when the mood in colleges is so changed that students will demand the personal attention of professors as something for which they have paid. They may come to see that a professor is cheating if he simply comes to class, gives his lecture or demonstration, and then hurries away by the back door, not to be seen for the next two days. Students who understand something of the gravity of our world situation might reasonably be angry if their professors do poor and shoddy teaching and give their students no personal attention. The present high rates of tuition may hasten this development.

Since good teaching is a task which requires so much energy and imagination, the college community should be so arranged as to provide each professor with the conditions in which such powers can be expected to develop. There should be times when the professor is available, but a man cannot be at his best when he *is* available unless there are also times when he is *not* available. One of the greatest collegiate inventions is that of the long summer vacation. Students may not need it, especially in the light of the radical shift from the farm work which was originally envisioned, but the instructors most certainly do. A man may engage for twelve months a year on machine-tool work, with only a short vacation, without impairment of his powers, but he cannot do the same as a teacher. During the main part of the year the nervous output of a good teacher is so tremendous that there must be a period of intake. "Three to four months free, without imposed obligations, is a strict minimum for all teachers," says one who is himself a famous teacher.[5]

Our present danger is the danger of losing the precious spark. Because it is more economic to do so, many colleges now operate

[5] Jacques Barzun, *Teacher in America* (New York, 1945), p. 257n.

the year round and instructors frequently teach all summer as well as the rest of the year. How terrible if teachers are forced to start the autumn semester already fatigued! When this becomes the general practice the college has simply become even more like a factory, presenting, accordingly, most of the evils of factory life. There is a good argument for using college facilities in the summer, but when we do so we shall insist, providing we care about great teaching, which is fresh teaching, that those who teach in the summer have a comparable period of freedom from imposed obligations at some other period of the year. This is most easily done by institutions which operate on the four-quarter system.

We must likewise be careful, in our effort to maintain good teaching, to see to it that instructors are not too greatly burdened with work on committees. Committees may be necessary elements in any democratic procedure, but everyone recognizes them as wasters of time and energy. The solution is to have fewer and better committees, with many decisions made administratively by people who are not trying to teach and who enjoy administrative work. Probably each professor should serve on one committee, so as to keep in touch with the ongoing events of the academic community, but more than this entails danger to the very enterprise which the committees exist to foster. We cannot expect great teaching if we also make our professors into chore boys, with so many duties that no energy is left for the creative thinking without which the art of teaching cannot be perfected.

If we see good teaching as our pearl of great price, two important conclusions follow, one negative and the other positive. The negative conclusion is that we dare not keep a man on the teaching staff when he is a poor teacher, however loyal he is to the college. If he has served for years, the college undoubtedly owes him something, but it would be mistaken kindness to let this claim loom so large that we forget at the same time the valid claim of the students who are being cheated by dull or spiritless or unplanned teaching. Dull teaching is a luxury which the college cannot afford. The reason the college cannot afford it is that, for the college, teaching is at the center of the created community. In a college the teacher cannot be hidden. This is not so true in some great universities which can place men in positions so obscure that they do little harm and, in any case, are lost in the faceless academic crowd.

There are some good things which can be said for academic tenure, but it is important also to say that it involves much that is patently evil. The chief practical effect of tenure is to protect the incompetent. On the whole the ablest men are not concerned with tenure at all and certainly do not wish to remain a minute where they are not wanted. Probably we shall need to maintain tenure because of the security it gives to men who espouse unpopular causes, but even that battle is now largely a thing of the past. In many institutions today the men most secure in their positions are those who hold supposedly radical opinions, because, even though they are incompetent, the authorities hesitate to dismiss them for fear of a hue and cry about academic freedom. What we must seek to avoid, in the academic profession, is the kind of security which insures the same rewards for the able and the inept.

The positive conclusion is that the college must seek to find brilliant teachers wherever they may be found and must give this task of selection real priority. The addition of an enkindling teacher is a matter of such importance that it justifies overloading a department or even unbalancing a budget. Excellent teachers are so rare that they must be taken when found. David Starr Jordan sometimes discovered his best men on a train journey and hired them en route. Subsequent experience justified his rashness in nearly every instance.

The classic American example of how to give priority to the nature of the *man* is that provided by the great Timothy Dwight, when he was president of Yale College. Because President Dwight felt the need of instruction in chemistry, he looked around the country as best he could, but was not able to find any available chemistry scholar who also appealed to him as a potentially brilliant teacher. Chemists, of course, were not then numerous. Finally President Dwight fastened upon Benjamin Silliman, a young man of exceptional promise, who was only twenty-three years of age, and who had never seen a chemistry experiment. He employed this young man as professor of chemistry in Yale College and sent him away to study, at the expense of the college, in order that he might learn chemistry. The young man returned, gave his first lecture when he was twenty-five, and built up one of the leading chemistry departments in the nation. Today one of the colleges of Yale University bears this scholar's name.[6]

Dwight was running some risk, but he rightly thought that the risk he took was less than the risk of apparent security, at the price of dullness or mediocrity. In the actual event, his judgment was justified. But he would not have made his gamble if he had not had his philosophy straight. He knew that the real assets of a college are not buildings or systems, but *men*. He knew that the teacher is an enkindler and that the test of his success lies in the kind of fire he lights. The greatness of any college is directly proportional to the number of its teachers who are truly effective in this sacred function. President Dwight understood the function because he was one who performed it well, even while he was president. Much of his secret lay in the fact that he was never bored with the task of dealing with questions old to him, but new to students. It could be truly said of Dwight that "no matter how often he had heard a class dispute the same question, if it involved some vital truth which he thought this group should see clearly, he kindled to it as warmly and eloquently as to an important public address."[7]

The college which understands both its meaning and its potential greatness will not only be bold in its search for men who can

[6] See Charles E. Cuningham, *Timothy Dwight* (New York: The Macmillan Company, 1942), pp. 197ff.

[7] *Ibid.*, p. 246. In this connection see also Ralph Henry Gabriel, *Religion and Learning at Yale* (New Haven: Yale University Press, 1958), Chapter IV.

teach; it will also insist that the good teacher be adequately rewarded. In some institutions it may be right and just to base advancement merely upon the publication of research, but it would be wrong to do this in a college. There are men who have never published anything and yet are tremendous assets because of the way in which they give themselves without stint to their students. This kind of excellence is not something which can be measured mechanically, but it is reasonably obvious to anyone who will take the trouble to try to observe it. Note which teachers the former students seek out upon their return; note which teachers inspire their students to do scholarly work; note whose help is sought in human crises. Even though the good teacher has his best rewards already, because they are intrinsic, the college ought also to encourage what he is trying to accomplish by the incentive of advancement and by providing at least enough salary to allow him to teach with an undivided mind.

One of the greatest dangers facing the modern American college is the danger of expansion. The temptation is to proliferate with new departments and even more buildings, to the neglect of the one thing needful. We cannot eliminate the temptation but we can, at least, gather strength to meet it by reminding ourselves of the nature of our best tradition and by heeding the wise words of some of our best scholars. One of the clearest voices has been that of Carl L. Becker, who wrote, more than forty years ago, "You may have the finest material plant and still have a very poor university; whereas, if you have a good faculty of able scholars and teachers you will have a good university even with inferior buildings and equipment." [8] Some factors change with the changing of civilization, but the centrality of the good teacher does not change.

[8] Carl L. Becker, *Detachment and the Writing of History*, p. 146.

IV

The Student

"When a multitude of young persons, keen, open-hearted, sympathetic, and observant, as young persons are, come together and freely mix with each other, they are sure to learn from one another, even if there be no one to teach them."

CARDINAL NEWMAN

IMPORTANT as the teacher is, his importance would recede into nothingness, apart from the existence of students. There are excellent scholarly institutions without students, but the college is not one of them. The entire college exists for the sake of producing significant changes in the lives of the men and women who enter the community voluntarily in the hope of personal improvement and consequent effectiveness. Some, unfortunately, are not improved; indeed, some are actually made worse by the experience. Sometimes the students lose whatever sense of meaning their lives have had earlier and they leave with deeply ingrained habits of laziness or self-indulgence. But, at the same time, there are others who, in the midst of the experience, take hold of their own lives in a wholly new way. Some bloom early; some, as a result of the college experience, actually become new persons; many engage in periods of wholesome self-criticism. It is these who justify the entire effort, but they do not constitute the only justification. Part of the justification is based upon the experience of those who show little gratitude and no intelligent response while in college, but who, because of the influences which the college makes possible, develop their potentialities later. The fact that the unconscious influences may not show their effects until there has been a passage of years does not mean that they are, for that reason, ineffective.

The saddest feature of contemporary college life is involved in the fact that thousands of students resist all of the helpful inflences for the simple reason that they do not really want to be in college. They may want to live in a fraternity house or they may want to attend college dances, but they do not really desire membership in the total intellectual community which the college is. Why, then, are they present? Chiefly because they are *sent*. And they are sent because college attendance is now a status operation, especially helpful to the social standing of the parents. When a boy is expelled for poor work or bad conduct, the real sufferer is not the boy but his mother, who has to impart the sad news to the other members of her literary club on Friday afternoon. The best people in modern America send their children to college and, if they can pass the entrance hurdles, they send them to the best colleges. This is simply part of contemporary culture.

The status appeal is one of the major reasons for the contemporary college boom, but the college pays a high price for such prestige value. Every professor knows what it is to face, in any large class, a good many who are digging their heels in, with the manifest intention of resisting knowledge as long as possible. When the teacher is really competent and persuasive, these young people have a hazardous task, for there is always a chance that they may be caught by his enthusiasm. They may begin to read Plato and consequently become truly interested in ideas. If they are to succeed in remaining uninterested, they must be continually on their guard, but in this effort some show remarkable skill, and a minority are able to hold out to the bitter end. To these the emphasis on the intellectual life seems fundamentally unfair. It is the one blot on an otherwise rosy and pleasant scene. They naturally desire the college social life and the prestige of attendance, but what a shame to have all this marred by study!

If anyone thinks this is a caricature, he merely shows thereby that his experience with colleges is severely limited. There is no way of knowing with accuracy what the proportions are, but there is reason to believe that the resisters of knowledge constitute a large minority, if not a majority, of attenders. The bills are high, but Dad joyfully pays them, even though there must be family sacrifices to accomplish this. College is so good, he thinks, that it is worth some personal hardship on his part. On the other hand, thousands of students are not aware that sacrifices are being made on their behalf. Some do not even know what their college years cost. If told that their parents have spent $10,000 on their education in four years of loafing, some hardly believe it.

The basic trouble is that in our social system we have allowed higher education to become a right rather than a privilege. It is no longer something which young people desire so deeply that they gladly work hard to save in order to attend and work to earn while studying. In many ways college life was more valued when it was harder to get. All admirers of Franklin's *Autobiography* will remember the passages about his youth in Boston when he was eager for learning in spite of poor opportunities. While his brother and the other employees went from the printing house to their meals, young Benjamin Franklin stayed behind to eat a light lunch of his own preparation, so that he had the rest of the time until their return for study. A passage which is almost incomprehensible to many modern students is the following:

I took Cocker's book of arithmetic and went through the whole by myself with great ease. I also read Seller's and Shermy's books of navigation, and became acquainted with the little geometry they contain; but never proceeded far in that science. And I read about this time Locke "On Human Understanding," and the "Art of Thinking," by Messrs. du Port Royal.

At the same time young Franklin counted himself lucky to have some opportunity to study in the fields of grammar, rhetoric,

and logic and to be introduced to Socratic method by Xenophon's
Memorabilia. It is a shocking thing to say, but it is true, that the
poor printer's assistant actually got a better education in his scraps
of time than do many modern youths who live for four years in
beautiful colleges with large libraries, helpful professors, and every
opportunity for advancement. The entire difference, of course,
is the difference in motive. We are not likely to get far, however
fine our facilities, if the desire to learn is absent. Knowledge is
something which men and women are able to resist if they will.

The solution to this problem will have to come by a variety of
approaches, but the most important method is that of a more
careful selection of applicants. The present situation is favorable
in that the number of applicants is, in most places, greater than
the number who can be accepted. In the popular excitement
over education, it is commonly stated that colleges must accept
more students because of the increase in the number of applicants.
This is a strange conclusion, because it cannot be valid except
on the assumption that all who apply should be admitted. That
this is the case is by no means obvious. Of course it is true that
more applications are made than can be accepted, but it would
be tragic for the college, in response to this flood, to ruin itself
by such bigness that it would change its entire character and no
longer do for *any* what most needs to be done. The alternative is
tough-mindedness in selection. The sober truth is that a great
many who are now in college ought not to be there at all, and
many who make application for admission ought to be steered
elsewhere, into pursuits more congenial to them or more suitable
to their needs. Thousands are wasting time in college who might
be living really productive lives if they were engaged in industry.

When the wrong people go to college, harm is done in several
specific ways. In the first place, the student himself is harmed
because he often develops habits of laziness and superficiality
which may remain with him a long time. In the second place, the
whole college is harmed because each malcontent influences

others. In the third place, harm is done to some potential student who might have been accepted if the quota had not already been filled by the addition of some who do not belong in college life at all. In the fourth place, the nation is deprived of part of the labor force it needs when young men and women with no real interest in intellectual development are maintained in relative idleness and self-indulgence in the years of their greatest physical energy. If a young person in college is not interested, and if there is something else he would rather do, his parents and advisers would be wise to urge him to go do it. Anything is better than a life devoid of interest and incentive. Perhaps, in later years, some keen interest will be aroused and then the student originally unfitted for college life may come back to it a different person and profit by it remarkably. This has occurred many times, some of the best experience academically coming after a few years of military service and consequent growth in maturity.

Though the state universities may be required to accept all citizens who are high school graduates, the independent colleges are not under the same necessity, either legally or morally. They can *choose*, and the right choice of students is bound to be, more and more, crucial to their total success. But on what basis shall the choice be made? Sometimes, in the recent past, the choice has been made almost wholly in the light of intelligence tests or on College Board examinations, but such methods are far from perfect. They certainly keep out some students who would profit greatly by what the college offers and they permit some to enter whose only real qualification has been attendance at a good secondary school. Sometimes those with the highest intelligence quotients become the most unsatisfactory students, while, on the other hand, some of the best students, judged by all-round development, are those who before entrance showed more promise than actual achievement.

Those who conduct admissions offices need to have almost superhuman judgment. Since it is obvious that the decisions about admission cannot be made by a machine or by some formula, there is always an element of risk and there will, consequently, be some failures. In the nature of things, some who are admitted will fail to profit by what the college has to give or to add to the worth of the community. All that we have a right to demand of admission officers is a reasonably high record of success in choosing persons. But we must make the director of admissions know how important his work is. He and the president can make or break the institution, for he selects the students and the president selects the instructors.

What the officers of admissions must look for is, first, a real desire for an education, and, second, some promise of leadership in the enterprise. It would be a shame, when there are not enough academic opportunities to go around, to waste any on those who do not care or who demonstrate no real promise of achievement. The students admitted will not be perfect and they will not already be fully developed in their powers, for the college exists to aid in this development, but what we need is the work of wise men who, to paraphrase the words of William James already used, will know a student of promise when they see him. In judgment of this kind, ability to judge attitude is central. We must watch for a willingness to learn, a willingness to be taught, and the conviction that college life is a great privilege.

Another way in which we can profit by better motives is that of the frequent explanation of the situation to those who have already been admitted. The fact that the president and the professors know what a college is trying to accomplish does not mean that the students know. Accordingly there can be a wide use of assemblies to explain the entire undertaking. The small areas of the map are often confusing until the larger map is unfolded. On the whole, people do better work, even in a factory, if they understand something of the total process, and a college community is far more responsive to this kind of explanation than is that of a factory. A college president must take the responsibility of presenting, as ably as he can, the educational philosophy on which the college operates. One reason why the first Timothy Dwight was so successful at Yale was that he spoke to the students so often. It is unfortunate that in some modern colleges the students hardly recognize the president when they see him.

The problem of motivation is largely solved if students come to think of themselves as part of an ongoing tradition. The student at Davidson can be helped by realizing that Woodrow Wilson once studied where he now studies. When this sense of membership in a continuing heritage becomes part of a student's conscious experience, great things may happen. He not only moves over from the supposition that attendance at college is his right to the consciousness of sharing in a high privilege; he goes farther and begins to share a sense of responsibility for the continuation and augmentation of an already valuable heritage. A college at its best thus becomes not merely a society, but a responsible society.

A sad feature of our present college life is that in some cases the professors do almost all of the work. Indeed students often think of their major or sole responsibility as that of attending classes, forgetting that in the class hour it is the professor and not the student who is expending energy. Often the student is only a passive receiver of what the professor has prepared with arduous care and has delivered with brilliance. The main work of the student must be done elsewhere, and the lecture, however brilliantly delivered, has little permanent value unless this student work is done. Attending class may be important, but it is among the least difficult of the good student's responsibilities. In the contemporary college there is too much teaching and not enough learning! We must find a way to reduce the number of class hours, so that the student who wishes to make a good use of his time can have unbroken hours for mature intellectual labor on his own. If not, the unequal effort of the teacher is largely wasted.

Though attendance at class is not work, in the full sense of the word, students can learn a great deal about the right use of such opportunities, and it is the duty of the college to show how this may be accomplished. In most classes a student gets a great deal more out of the presentation or discussion if he takes notes constantly. The reason for this is that reception is even better when there is action. Usually there is no genuine *impression* unless there is *expression*, and writing is a good form of expression. The chief value of taking notes is that the student thereby ceases to be merely passive. The best notes are not stenographic accounts of all that is said, but rather a continual digest, in which each paragraph of the lecturer is reduced to two or three sentences in the student's book, but all is made consecutive, orderly, and smooth. This kind of note-taking is a great art and can produce something of considerable importance for later years. All of the major writings of Aristotle were produced in this way and thus the essence of the great teacher's contribution was saved for posterity. The girl who merely sits or even knits is not only insulting the lecturer; she is likewise spoiling her own opportunity. Of all educational paradoxes the strangest lies in the fact that people are continually willing to pay for education and then do their best not to get value received. Not satisfied with being cheated, students deliberately arrange to cheat themselves.

Not only will the good student learn to take notes in classes; he will also learn to keep his own commonplace book in which he records his ideas, quotations from general reading, and summaries of the ideas of others which seem to him worth preserving. This is one of the chief ways in which a student can begin to enter into genuine intellectual maturity. At the same time he can be developing a personal library, spending a little money when he has it to buy books that he expects to prize as long as he lives. These will seldom be textbooks and will often be works which can be had for little because they now appear profusely in inexpensive reprints. A college which cares about this important aspect of the life of its students will provide a campus bookstore, by no means limited to works which are required in particular classes. A wise student will keep a list of books which he hopes to buy and certainly to read when opportunity offers. The character of this list is one measure of the quality of his education. Later, when he is able to visit bookstores, particularly secondhand bookstores, in various cities, he can purchase the books most desired. Sometimes the best of education comes after college and before family responsibilities have begun, when the student can enjoy the books of which he has heard in college, but could not then find time to read. The student is using his valuable college years wisely, and thus making them more valuable, if he recognizes them as a beginning of what he expects to fulfill in subsequent years.

Of late the word duty has largely gone out of use in academic areas, partly because of a superficial conception of tolerance. Perhaps, now that we are living in sterner times, we may come to realize that some things are intolerable and that a world without the valid appeal to duty is a poor world in which to exist. The student should be convinced that because his opportunities are great, his duties are correspondingly great. Many persons, through many years, have produced this college inheritance into which the contemporary student enters with so little appreciation. Others made possible the collection of books; others established the standards of scholarship; others sacrificed to build the halls of residence in which he can live in comparative luxury. All of this adds up to a tremendous moral responsibility. The chief responsibility is that of making a good use of the facilities that are provided, for that is all that the donors ever require if they understand what they are doing.

Few changes could be more significant than a change in regard to the student's conception of what he is and who he is. Much of our expensive undertaking is a failure so long as the average student thinks of himself as an adolescent, even though one who is fully grown. What is desirable is to help students in college to look upon themselves as persons in early maturity, rather than persons in late childhood. This, of course, cannot be done all at once; but if all who care make it their aim, much may be accomplished. The marks of adolescence in college are evident for all to see. One is the fear of being friends with professors, the chief fear being that the fellow students will tease. A mature person would not care in a situation of this character, whether he were teased or not. A second mark of adolescence is the determination to do as little as possible in order to satisfy requirements. A mature student would look upon his instruction as a marvelous opportunity which might not come again and he would try to make the most of it. Almost never would he be concerned with his grades, because his full attention would be given to the question of whether he were accomplishing anything in his chosen study. If a young man is studying the Russian language, with an eye to possible diplomatic service later, he is a fool to be deeply concerned about the mark in the registrar's office. The rational thing for him to be concerned about is whether he can learn to read, to speak, and to write a language which is bound to be increasingly important in his generation.

The average college student is really capable of accomplishing far more than almost any contemporary student accomplishes. His body is as large as it will ever be, and this includes his physical brain. He is in a period of great bodily vitality, usually with no debilitating diseases, and he is given splendid opportunities for exercise which improves his general fitness. Moreover, he is normally free from family cares, so that he can give his mind to his work with a singleness which is usually impossible during long periods of his subsequent career. His capacity for hard work is usually greater than he knows. Even when we grant that Blaise Pascal was a man of unusul powers, it is revealing to the college man to realize that Pascal was doing some of his best scholarly work when he was at the age of a college sophomore of our time. It is good that the student should be reminded of men of this character who proved the possibility of accomplishing mature work in early years. The work of Lord Bryce in the study of government is a shining example, but it is by no means unique.

If this idea of early maturity were really to take hold in our colleges, we should see an enormous change in a short time. Then there would be no lack of leadership, and responsibility would be widely shared. The college society would tend to become a real community and the work of the professors would be vastly improved because of the improved reception. Part of our failure now is fundamentally a failure of expectancy. We expect too little and we get what we expect.

There is a good chance that the present situation of competitive coexistence between the Communist world and ourselves may become a means of raising our sights. There is no doubt of its urgency and it is one which is likely to endure as long as we live. Actually it is a situation which we can accept with enthusiasm. If there is a real chance that the competition may express itself in ways other than destructive warfare, we are delighted. We accept the challenge to show which system is best in terms of art, of general culture, of the well-being of the total population, of science and letters. We have reason to believe that a society which permits freedom of thought is, in the long run, more productive in all of these areas than is any other of which we have heard. But just saying so is not enough. The point has to be demonstrated by writing better music and better books, by engaging more creatively in natural science, and by an educational system which has upon it the marks of manifest excellence. Some of the world's tragedy of lamentable divisions could be turned into a victory if only the students in our colleges could accept the Khrushchev challenge with both gaiety and seriousness.

One fine fruit of this development would be a growth in humility. We have abundant reason to be humble, now that we know we can be so markedly outclassed. All who think about the matter now know that we were wrong in our comfortable conviction that the members of a regimented society could not possibly produce as much scientifically or technically as do the members of a free society. What we overlooked was the quasi-religious drive of the Communist student, a drive which is more powerful than can be demonstrated by a people who have freedom but lack a burning faith. The truly beneficent result of the now widespread realization of the true situation is, then, that it has done something to give us humility. Students who are really humble are eager to learn because they realize how little they know. Much of the work of all professors who belong to the Socratic tradition has long been that of encouraging humility, as Socrates did for the slave in the *Meno,* but we may now be coming into a period of human history where events will do the humbling. This may give the professor more chance to begin the constructive part of his labor at once without the necessity of undermining the cocksureness which is such a formidable barrier to intellectual maturity.

The more we come to realize our need, the more certain we shall be to continue our education after the actual college attendance is ended. Today we keep accurate rolls of alumni, seeking to draw graduates into the ongoing life of the college. This is good, but it is not yet good enough. Too often the chief connection is merely financial or a matter of attendance at homecoming games. Insofar as we are really serious about competitive coexistence, we shall realize that our college *education* never rightly ends. It would be good if we should promote the idea of "once a member of a college, always a member." Ideally the bond is indissoluble. Therefore it is reasonable for those members no longer in residence to use college facilities year after year in acquiring reading lists, getting help on intellectual projects, and continuing education by correspondence. Any truly alert person needs to learn more than can be learned in four short years. Moreover, some of the best periods of learning come later, after more experience. With the postal system as good as it is, the unbroken contact is possible and ought normally to be part of our expectation.

The relation between the former student and the college may be a reciprocal one. Throughout the years the maturing member of the unbroken academic society may contribute as well as receive. If we develop enough imagination, we shall find many ways of using former students who will be valuable in what they can give residential students as a result of more experience. Completely new categories of academic service may be developed. It is a shame to limit connections to the trivial when they can be truly significant to all concerned.

The notion of education as an unending process can help the student to know what he has a right to expect from college. He will expect to receive some information, but he will understand that this is of minor importance in comparison to other possible gains. What the student must watch for, and what he has a right to expect, is the development of a habit of inquiry. This habit is most valuable if it includes a method by which any problem can be approached. The student who gets what college has to give learns to face a problem with analysis into its parts and with a calm appraisal of all possible hypotheses. He learns to move from the simple to the complex and he learns also to verify his conclusions insofar as they are verifiable. The point is that such a habit of method can be retained, long after the specific information is forgotten, precisely because it is put into continuous use. It thus becomes a means by which old information may be recovered or new information obtained. The emphasis on this point was one of the chief marks of the excellence exhibited in Newman's justly famous treatment of the central academic theme. Speaking of the undergraduate student, Newman wrote, "Let him once gain this habit of method, of starting from fixed points, of making his ground good as he goes, of distinguishing what he knows from what he does not know and I conceive he will be gradually initiated into the largest and truest philosophical views." [1]

[1] John Henry Newman, *On the Scope and Nature of University Education.* (Everyman Edition) Preface.

The wonder lies in the fact that what Cardinal Newman described can actually occur. The young man or woman, beginning to develop seriously such a "habit of method," frequently becomes a new person in a few weeks. Then, instead of resisting work, the liberated student is asking for more. Soon he embarks on some task in which he has a chance to know as much about some particular sector of knowledge as does any living person. Then the miracle has happened and the work is self-justifying. It is to produce changes of this kind that the college exists. Our shame, however, is that so many remain untouched all of their college days. Insofar as we recognize that students are important, we are unsatisfied with our present partial success in this major effort. We are grateful when the miracle occurs, but we must set the conditions for its greater frequency.

The only reasonable way to judge a college is not by the size of its campus or by the abundance of its financial resources or by the number of books in its library or even by the publications of its professors. The college is to be judged by the quality of its human product. The test of a successful college education is not to be found in the amount of knowledge which the graduates take away with them, most of which will be forgotten in any case, but rather by the appetite to know, by the determination to continue the educational process, and by the ability to think and act maturely. The purpose of a college is the production of persons who are both more civilized and more civilizing.

V

Administration

"Any college lives or dies by its appointments."
HOWARD LOWRY

THE administration of a college is a necessity. Though the Apostle Paul puts administrators in seventh place in his list of those with valuable gifts (I Cor. 12:28), administrators may be gratified that they are included somewhere. A president and his various administrative assistants, such as business managers, deans, directors of admissions, and secretaries of many kinds, are valuable, but they are valuable only instrumentally. They are successful, not when they draw attention to themselves, but when, by efficient operation and by wise decision, they make possible that which is intrinsically valuable. They exist to provide the means without which the ends will not be accomplished or accomplished so well.

Once our educational philosophy is centered upon the importance of the good teacher, we understand more easily the function of a president and his helpers. If there are to be good teachers, there must be someone to choose them; to support them in their struggles, especially when they espouse unpopular causes; and to see to it that they are, to some degree, liberated from the economic struggle so that they can give their time to their sacred undertaking with undivided attention. Moreover, the good teacher needs certain tools, particularly if he is operating in the natural sciences, and it is reasonable that these should be provided for him without undue effort on his part. All of this and much more of the same character is required if the community of learning and teaching is to operate efficiently, and the administrators are the persons assigned to such tasks. Modest though their calling is, in comparison with that of providing intellectual stimulation and guidance, we could not proceed well without them.

The development of the college presidency, as we know it, is relatively recent. Even a hundred years ago the college president presided over a modest office, with few helpers, and confined most of his energies to the lives of the students. He was their guide, their disciplinarian, and their friend. Being in most instances a clergyman, he was also their pastor and their most frequent chapel speaker. Often he taught at least one class. In any case his figure was familiar. Today, by contrast, there are college students who have never spoken to their President and even some who have never heard him speak. Instead of running the college with one secretary, as was once possible, the contemporary president has under his care a host of helpers and assistants, to whom most of the executive duties are delegated. Sometimes the administrative staff is almost as large as the teaching staff. After a certain size and complexity are reached, the problem of cutting down on this personnel is practically insoluble because more and more of the workers spend their time in service to one another. If there are many employees, somebody must write their checks, somebody must clean their offices, somebody must manage their coffee shop. The horrible thought has occurred that it would be possible to create an organization in which all the persons involved would be engaged in providing services for the organization itself, with no productive output whatever. Even when the students are absent during vacation time, many of the administrative responsibilities go on, exactly as in term time.

Now a college president, guiding, as he does, the destinies of so many people, has a heavy responsibility. His is the most significant voice concerning a budget which, annually, runs into more than a million dollars, even in a small college. In short he is conducting a big business, and he must see that it is conducted properly. It is no wonder that the ulcerated stomach is the president's chief occupational hazard. Because student tuition fees cannot be set at the level of the actual cost, the president and his delegates must always be raising money, either for capital funds or for current expenses or student scholarships. It sounds easy to say that a college should divide the annual budget by the number of students enrolled and make that figure the amount charged, but this direct method, apparently, will not succeed. The amount is so staggeringly large that the very students who would profit most from what the college has to give might then be kept away. Money must be given if equality of opportunity is to be achieved.

Equality of opportunity was provided in an earlier day by the relative ease with which an impoverished boy or girl could earn and study at the same time. The story of many prominent Americans involves, as a point of pride, work at waiting on table or doing other necessary tasks on the campus. The late J. P. McEvoy loved to tell how at Notre Dame he was a student-waiter who waited on student-waiters. "This, I respectfully submit," he said, "is the lowest form of collegiate life." Once, by using the summers profitably and by doing some work near the campus, it was possible for the industrious boy to earn his entire way through college and to graduate without any burden on his parents or any debt. The famous Dr. Carver, having been born into slavery and having no money at all, said later of his days at Simpson College that he realized there, for the first time, that he was a human being. Part of the reason for this was that the college, poor as it was in resources, helped him to earn his way. Good as this system of self-help was and much as we shall always cherish it, it is increasingly difficult to operate today. For one reason, the costs of higher education have risen much more than have general prices. The college which forty years ago charged $100 a year for tuition now charges at least $800, but our monetary inflation has not been, in this period, at the rate of eight to one. The real increase in cost has come about chiefly because modern education is far more complex and requires far more expensive equipment than was required forty years ago. But the added cost is not the only difficulty faced by those who would earn their way if they could. The organization of labor has made profitable summer work and even part-time work more difficult for the student to obtain. Most of the tasks the student would be glad to perform are already claimed by others who resent infringement on their domain.

It is because of the factors just mentioned that we need to adopt a policy to the effect that no student who is really a person of *promise* will ever be denied the opportunity for advanced education because of lack of funds. In a truly responsible society we shall look upon potential service as a pearl of great price, to be treated with reverential care. Brains are our real wealth, more today than ever. The scholarships arising out of federal funds and authorized by act of Congress will be a big help, but they cannot be sufficient. A great deal of voluntary giving will be required for as long in the future as we can see, providing we maintain the kind of society we claim to prize. For this reason alone we shall avoid, if we are wise, any tendency to despise the money-raising angle of college life. Money is important, not for its own sake, but because of what it can do for persons.

A president who accepts such a responsibility of management must often be absent from the campus. He will be away, not because he is shirking his college duties, but because he is performing them. He must visit foundations, give a multitude of speeches, attend regional meetings of alumni, share in educational conferences, approach leaders of industry, and watch constantly for prospective professors of the highest quality. As he is successful in all of these enterprises, which are connected intimately with his col-

lege duties, he is likely to be called upon for a variety of public
services, including those connected with the state and federal
governments. He is almost sure to be invited to become a member
of one or more national boards devoted to good causes. It is not
really surprising, therefore, if he is almost a stranger to his own students and even to some of his own instructors. Most presidents
regret their absence from the campus, wishing they could be present regularly to share in the local community life, but they are
drawn away against their wills. They wish, usually, that they could
teach at least one class, and a president before he takes office
often promises himself that he will do so, but the promise is found
to be difficult to keep. The demands are so urgent that continuity
of attention to teaching duties is practically impossible.

When we think of the variety of demands upon a college president, we are surprised that anyone can fill such an office with
distinction, yet it is often done. There are, of course, conspicuous
failures, which is not surprising, but we have a number of men who
perform presidential duties with admirable skill. To succeed they
do not have to be scholars of great repute, but they do have to
be persons who honor scholarship and who know a scholarly man
when they see him. What is required is a delicate balance between
a certain tough-mindedness which enables a man to say "No" if
a negative answer seems best for the good of all concerned and a
willingness to give other people both responsibility and authority
within their own fields of competence. A good academic leader
must be strong without being arbitrary.

A man will not, ordinarily, be a good college president if he is
greatly interested in being popular either with his professors or
with the students. Because the members of an academic community are human, sharing in all the evils and temptations of
human nature, troubles will arise. Jealousies will appear among
the faculty members and students will grow vociferous over supposed injustices or infringements of their liberties. The president
may sometime encounter an opposition so strong that he cannot

remove it, such as Woodrow Wilson experienced at Princeton, but in the long run a man will be honored for his stand on principle, regardless of the way in which the popular wind is blowing. Ray Lyman Wilbur, who was conspicuously strong in this regard, used to refer to what he called "the habit of decision." His rule was to *decide*, even though he was well aware that sometimes, because of human fallibility, he would make the wrong decision. His contention was that in most cases indecision involved a worse risk than decision, even though decision cannot be perfect. Indecision, Wilbur believed, is nearly always bad. The consequence was that a professor going to Dr. Wilbur with a problem got an answer, even though it was not the answer which he hoped to get. Then, in any case, the situation was clear and each man knew where he was. The professor's recommendation was either accepted or denied and he could proceed accordingly. Though the two men seem different in other ways, Ray Lyman Wilbur and Harry Truman had the characteristic of decisiveness in common. Speaking of the national presidency, Mr. Truman said, after he left office, "If he exercises his authority wisely, that is good for the country. If he does not exercise it wisely, that is too bad, but it is better than not exercising it at all."

One of the greatest dangers in modern college life is that of an extreme division of labor, especially when it creates too great a distinction between the teaching staff and the administrative staff. It is common on a campus to hear references to students, to faculty, and to administration, sometimes with the implied suggestion that these are essentially antagonistic groups, with different interests. Professors are particularly prone to refer to "the administration" as though referring to a different breed. Thus, sometimes, bitter antagonisms arise, and when there is a publicly recognized split along these lines, it does harm so great that it cannot be overcome in many years. The usual complaint of the teaching members against the administrative members of the academic community is that the latter are interested only in money or that scholarly integrity is being sacrificed in order to pacify certain elements of the outside community. Sometimes there is a little justification for this complaint, but more often the professor is curiously blind to his own interest and that of his teaching colleagues. Instead of resenting the effort to get money, he ought to be gratified; the effort makes a great difference in his own standard of living and that of his family.

As we understand the idea of a college better, we shall do all that we can to bridge any chasm which exists between administration and teachers and to avoid, if possible, its development. The chief way to do this is by the clear recognition that what we are producing is a *team*. Accordingly, the analogy with business, as it is usually understood, is a false analogy. At the present stage of industry it may be inevitable to have conference tables with labor representatives sitting on one side and management sitting on the other, but we want nothing remotely similar to this in a college. Nothing can be worse, academically, than the idea of a teachers' union, in which professors have the mentality of employees, with the notion that the owners and managers are their natural enemies. The Marxian analysis of the inevitability of class conflict has little bearing on contemporary industry, in which workers have fine cars and are nearly all capitalists of sorts, but it has no bearing at all on the academic situation.

If we see the entire staff as a team with a single purpose, then the president is the quarterback, but the point is that the quarterback is himself one of the participators in the game. All are engaged in one enterprise and all have the responsibility to help each other. Professors make a great mistake when they meticulously devote themselves to their teaching and refuse to engage in general activities that will help the total college life. My business, the professor may say, is to teach chemistry; therefore I shall not represent the college in public addresses or bother with the problem of admissions or with raising money. These are the tasks of men appointed for these purposes, the professor may think, and thus they are no responsibility of his. However common this attitude may be, it is harmful. The teacher who refuses to have any concern for the budget is like the player on the professional football team who knows that he is responsible for his end of the line, but cares nothing for what goes on at the other end. If the other end lets a runner get around him, that is just *his* hard luck and, if it happens very often, he won't be hired another year. However appropriate this attitude may be among hired men, it is wholly inappropriate among those engaged in producing an academic community, because they are not hired men. If they are in the business only for the salary or the prestige, they are in the wrong business. There is no possibility of making a really great college unless those who guide its destinies are committed men and women. What we seek, instead of a mechanical division of labor, is a fellowship of the concerned in which each *cares* about what his colleagues are doing and helps them when he can.

This changed conception would, if loyally accepted, do wonders to relieve the financial burden and to help to liberate the president of the college for other than merely financial duties. Every professor worth his salt has a multitude of connections and he might reasonably be watching for those in which he could bring together the desire to give to a really worthy end and the academic needs which he is bound to feel keenly. The way to succeed financially is for the entire team to feel the financial responsibility, both in reducing expenses and in increasing assets. Some of the finest gifts to colleges have come because of a potential giver's faith in some obscure professor and because the professor had the courage to make a suggestion or to follow a lead. The shame, however, is that this happens too rarely. It happens rarely, not because of any lack of potential donors, but because there are so many professors to whom the idea has never occurred. Some of those to whom it does occur reject it scornfully, as though an interest in getting money for the college would somehow besmirch them. Their attitude is comparable to that of European intellectuals who will not sully their hands by any physical labor, such as mowing a lawn or carrying luggage. The point is that in either case we have what is no more than an unattractive pose, which cannot be defended. The scholar who expects all of the practical work to be done by others, while he thinks his great thoughts, may have his place, but it is not in a college.

The financial responsibility is not the only practical one that ought to be widely shared in a college. A similar situation obtains in regard to the right selection of students. The temptation is to leave this problem to the director of admissions, with his secretarial staff and his testing equipment. After all, this is a professional job, in which there is no place for amateurs! Our job, the professors may say, is to teach them after they arrive, not to decide who comes. There is plausibility in this familiar position, but in practice it is harmful. If the college is to be what it ought to be, fulfilling the promises implied in accepting gifts, it must have in it the right students. Actually it is far easier to get the money than it is to keep the promises which acceptance of money involves. It is a difficult matter to build up the right student body, which is a body made up of those who can truly profit by what the college has to offer. The answer to this problem is never a perfect one, and mistakes will always be made, but the best answer lies in a sharing of the responsibility. The wise professor will, as he travels, always be watching for potential students of the particular kind which his college exists to serve. He can find them in his vacations and wherever he goes. A chance conversation on a train or plane or ship may be the key factor in guiding some young person into a higher education. Far from it being unsuitable for professors to engage in such recruitment, they are the very ones whom the young persons ought to meet if prospective students are to understand what the college means. It may be much more impressive to a young person to discuss college with a distinguished professor than to talk with a field representative of the admissions office.

If professors have responsibility in the selection of students, they likewise have responsibility in finding new professors. Able as the president may be, he cannot know all of the people he ought to know, especially among those who could develop into brilliant teachers. He must have some help, and where can this help be more intelligent than in his own teaching staff? The idea is for all who care to be watching all the time for new resources, both human and physical, in order to bring an ever greater vitality into the total enterprise. There is no incompatibility between the conception that each tries to do a superior job in his own specific area and the parallel conception that each must feel a responsibility for the whole. The paradox is the ancient one that each must bear his own burden, but, at the same time, all must bear the burdens of others.

While this paradox is a Christian idea, it need not be limited to a specially Christian institution, but applies to any college which understands its vocation. It is essential to their nature that colleges, of whatever type, be "committed communities." By using this terminology, says Professor Calhoun, "we intend to say they are corporate bodies whose members represent wide variety and at the same time deep-going unity, and freedom of a radical sort that is self-disciplined. We are talking of communities committed to distinctive ends of their own." If we keep in mind the nature of our commitment, we are providing, thereby, the best antidote to the specialization which leads to sheer anarchy. Calhoun's warning, at this point, is highly relevant.

We human beings carry both our limitations and our sinfulness into academic relationships. We tend to become defensive and prideful about what we regard as peculiarly our own possession and contribution, and the temptation is always present to disparage our neighbor in the interest of exalting and validating ourselves. Yet if there is to be genuine community of life and learning, it seems to be plain that diversity must go hand in hand with at least that measure of unity that displays itself in some degree of common understanding and of common respect one for another.[1]

[1] Robert L. Calhoun, "Christian Vocation on the College Campus," *The Christian Scholar*, Vol. XXXVII, pp. 271, 272.

One of the best results of the acceptance of the idea of community, with its consequent stress on the work of a team, on which the president is only one member, though a valuable one, is that by loyalty to this idea we can reduce the size of the administrative staff. For years we have been moving in the direction of greater expense for administrative salaries, in comparison to salaries for teachers, but now we may be able to reverse this process. The best administrators are eager, not to enlarge their relative importance, but to reduce their duties. One of the most successful of college presidents, O. P. Kretzmann, of Valparaiso, is taking the lead in the effort to reduce the administrative overhead, with its too many deans and too many managers. "I believe," he says, "that the Christian college in America should take the lead in de-emphasizing the importance of administration. Many functions now conducted by presidents and deans should be returned to our faculties. The Christian College is in a uniquely fortunate position to do this. Our relation to our teaching colleagues is not as employer to employee, nor even as partners in a great and common enterprise. It is much higher and greater and deeper than that." [2]

What is a college? Sometimes students suppose that *they* are the college, but of course in this they are wrong. The college also includes those who teach, those who guide, those who support. It includes former members as well as present members and it certainly includes those who are the legal trustees. Sometimes, in recent years, the members of college boards of trustees have not seemed to amount to much except to keep up the legal amenities and to provide a bit of window dressing. Some boards have been essentially yes men for the president and have been appointed with that in mind. Along with the hard-working and deeply committed board members there have been others who have received appointment, not because of any expectation of real service, but because their names add luster to the enterprise.

[2] O. P. Kretzmann, "Administration in the Christian College," *Towards a Christian Philosophy of Higher Education* (Philadelphia: The Westminister Press, 1957), p. 137.

One of the beneficent results of serious rethinking about the nature of a college is that we are taking more seriously the role of a trustee. There is, indeed, a good deal of reason to take the role seriously. When we consider the expense of the operation, the seriousness of the purpose, and the great national need, it is clear that those who guide the destinies of colleges carry heavy responsibilities. They constitute the final academic court of appeal, they usually make the major appointments, and they certainly determine over-all policy. In the early days of American education they did still more. At what is now Washington and Lee, for example, the trustees conducted the examinations at the end of the year, setting the questions and judging the results. In this way they had a reasonably accurate check not only upon the work of the students but, even more important, on the work of the professors. This precise task is not likely to be undertaken today, partly because many trustees would not feel qualified to perform it, but we are at least moving back toward a position of great responsibility. We are beginning to have offers of advanced instruction for trustees as well as for presidents, and this, once started, may grow in importance and scope.

It is certainly not sufficient for members of a board of trustees to attend meetings three times a year, vote to accept with gratitude the president's report and the proposals of the executive committee, and then go home, to be seen no more until the next meeting. There has been so much of this procedure that, even in colleges, the professors and the trustees do not know one another, while many students never see a trustee in their entire college career. This must change. Trustees cannot vote intelligently about college policies unless they know the college at first hand. In order to know it they must sit in some classes, listen to lectures, enter into discussions at the snack bars, and visit students in their rooms. If the occupant of an important professorial chair is to be named, the man appointed has a right to believe that he has the informed backing of those who have made the appointment. Most professors would welcome the attendance of trustees at their lectures and would by no means suspect snooping. In the same way most professors are delighted if the president, out of his busy life, finds time to attend classes and thus see, at first hand, what is going on. The more imagination they put into their work, the more pleased they are to have their work observed. Almost any class, with the possible exception of the small seminar, is improved by the presence of visitors. The work seems more important to the students if it seems important to others, while, in any case, the professor's own sights are raised.

Some trustees are men and women so occupied with their own private duties that they cannot give much time to public responsibilities, but it is doubtful if a person should accept appointment on a college board if he cannot spend at least three or four days a year in actual residence at the college. When men are far enough along in their own work that they can be retired or semiretired, the opportunity for a closer connection is immense. College management can become, for such men, their other vocation, dignifying their free years and bringing untold strength to the college. Such men, needing no remuneration, may be far more valuable than anyone who could be hired, yet they cost the college nothing. Since we are stronger, on the whole, than our ancestors were at the time of retirement, there are many good years available, in which the college profits by a wealth of experience and consequent soundness of judgment. The advantage to be gained by professors with such wise and experienced men as personal counselors is potentially great. The college would be wise to provide guest rooms, constantly available to trustees, and work out some system of rotation so that some members of the governing body are nearly always in residence.

The use of retired men in this way would take many burdens off the shoulders of younger men and thus liberate them for the duties, especially those of a scholarly nature, for which they are eager to find time. Some of the committee work which is so harassing to professors could be done by the dedicated visitors who, because they are officially retired, have a great deal of time and are not so likely to feel restive under the pressure of committee responsibilities. What is more important, however, is for board members simply to sit with professors and discuss their work. A professor often needs someone to care about what he is doing, to listen critically to his plans, and to help him with ideas. Frequently he has no one to go to in this fashion because the president is busy and his colleagues are buried under their own work.

We have as yet hardly scratched the surface in what can be gained from people in retirement, and especially academic retirement. Often when a professor retires at the age of sixty-five or seventy, he feels bereft because all of his former responsibilities in the college are suddenly ended. He is no longer on any committees; he has no duties; he frequently has the forlorn feeling of being no longer needed. There is a consequent emptiness or even resentment in his own life, while the institution he loves is deprived of what he has to give. There he sits in his own home, sad because he is no longer needed, while his younger former colleagues are overburdened with details, many of which he would be glad to handle. The path of wisdom would be to look upon the retired professors as persons constituting a "senate," a group, that is, marked by experienced wisdom, which can serve to liberate others from overwork.

The arguments for retirement are, for the most part, sound. For one thing, it is good to pass on some places of importance to new men before these men are of advanced age themselves. Furthermore, the day will come when a man is not as able to teach as he once was, and since he may be incapable of judging this himself, it is good to have a rule applied which is applied at all. But retirement need not mean cessation, and if we are wise will not mean this. Retirement, we see more and more, is freedom to engage in new and somewhat different tasks. The retired faculty members need not and ought not to have the same duties which they had when in active service. One useful new service which the retired teachers might perform would be that of acting as a senior cabinet for the president. In this capacity they could render their judgment on prospective professors, give advice in college publications, and even take over some of the time-consuming duties, such as the preparation of the catalogue. By being drawn into college life again such men would feel free to talk with students and could have more unhurried time for student contacts than can the teaching professors, who often feel forced to break off a potentially fruitful conference to read papers that must be returned the next day. The older man, brought back in this informal way, may have chances to do those things which he always wanted to do earlier and could not do for lack of time. The older and more unhurried but wise men, sitting like academic Bernard Baruchs on the campus benches, might come to be an accepted and valued part of the campus scene. All of this and much more will follow, once the managers of a college come to see retirement as the opening of new doors and not the closing of doors. The Whitney Foundation has already shown imagination in helping to place men in institutions other than their own, but not enough has been done to maintain the connection in the place where it means most.

The entire financial arrangement of the independent college, with its annual appeals and its inevitable emphasis upon public relations, is not anything of which we need to be ashamed. It is closely allied with one of the good things in western civilization, voluntary support of public services. This is by no means standard in the world, some countries having no service organizations at all. By good fortune our civilization grew in a time when the voluntary contribution of time and money seemed the natural thing. On the American frontier, if hospitals or academies were to be built, the citizens got together and built them. There was no easy way to tap a federal or state treasury, and this was fortunate because it developed self-reliance, or, more accurately, voluntary group responsibility. There are nations today in which all higher education is paid for by the state, precisely as are roads and military establishments, but we have been saved, by voluntary philanthropy, from the worst features of academic beauracracy. Our proudest boast, therefore, is that we are producing a responsible society. Even the state universities do not rely merely upon taxation, but solicit large funds, particularly for the construction of buildings and for scholarship purposes.

We have had in the middle period of the twentieth century a manifest boom in the construction of college buildings. Much of this has been both necessary and wise, partly because not enough new buildings were constructed during the great depression and during the Second World War. Now that we have the new buildings, however, it is time to call a halt. Of course it is easier to procure money for a building than for anything else, because the donor has something for his money which he can see, and because buildings lend themselves so easily to memorial purposes. It would be easy to go on building, but it would be wrong to do so, because what is needed now is an educational program of such excellence that it justifies the buildings. It is easier to concentrate upon means than upon ends, but it is a dangerous temptation. The result is the giantism of the great plant, which can easily be a burden rather than a help in the major undertaking. Each new building means added labor and added expense for upkeep, which means added administrative staff. Soon we can reach a point where the operation is topheavy.

The way of excellence now lies, not in allowing the proliferation of construction and activities to go on, but in an attempt to consolidate forces and to concentrate on fewer aims. We need to do few things and to do them better. Instead of increasing the physical plant, we need to consider ways of using more fully what we already have. To this end, the vacation system needs a genuine overhauling. It is evident that, for the most creative teaching, the professor needs at least three months of freedom each year, to think and read and to write, but the student does not need this much. As remunerative summer employment becomes more difficult to obtain, it is a waste of human resources for grown young people to spend all of the summer in self-indulgence. The solution of this problem does not necessarily consist in college residence for four quarters a year, but may consist, instead, in guided summer experiences which are calculated to have something of the function of laboratory work. Ordway Tead maintains that "The educational experience, direction and control should occupy approximately eleven months of the year and not eight. It should clearly include exposures and activities which are more than bookish. The longer college year would offer the needed chance for first-hand contact with the soil through agricultural work, with city life through urban work experience, with special community problems in rural, small city and metropolitan areas." [3]

One important resource in administration, heretofore largely unexploited, is that involved in the use of able students as advisers to the president. In most cases the students who are nearing the end of their campus residence have about as accurate a sense of the worth of the various instructors as anyone is likely to have. Experience shows that such students can be trusted to keep confidences and to take the responsibility of honest judgment seriously. Often they can answer questions about professors more accurately than can the colleagues of these professors, particularly because the colleagues have never observed them in the teaching role. If, as the president of Wooster has pithily remarked, a college "lives or dies by its appointments," the appointments made by an administrator are his most crucial acts and he needs all of the informed and loyal help he can get. Though we have long had student government, the use of students in an advisory capacity goes far beyond what has usually been envisaged. Administration becomes better when it is broadly based.

[3] Ordway Tead, "Why Liberal Colleges Tomorrow," *Amherst Graduates Quarterly*, Vol. XXXIII, No. 1, p. 3.

VI.

Curriculum

"What we do not teach we cannot save."
NELSON ROCKEFELLER

THE quality of those who teach is more important, in a college, than is the selection of subjects. A new-fashioned curriculum will not make up for mediocre teaching. The president of Barnard has said this is a way to arrest attention. "I submit," she says, "that the actual *content* of courses is not so important as the *method* by which it is presented; that the material of the curriculum is insignificant in comparison with the quality of those who teach." [1] This brilliant educator, who has served at Bryn Mawr as well as Barnard, goes on to point out that Thomas Arnold of Rugby was extremely successful in his product, "not through expensive integrated courses," but "through the sheer force of his own conviction and the clarity of his own goals." To one who asked earnestly what he taught, so that he might choose between the courses, Whitehead is supposed to have replied, with equal earnestness, "I teach three courses, Whitehead I, Whitehead II, and Whitehead III."

Once we have reaffirmed the principle of the supremacy of the teacher, it is worth while to consider the right selection of courses

[1] Millicent C. McIntosh, *Education for What?* (Stamford, Conn., The Overbrook Press, 1948), p. 6.

80

in a college, because, though a great teacher can glorify any, and a poor teacher can spoil any, some studies are more appropriate than others. Certainly we cannot defend, with any rationality, the practice of allowing students to choose all of their studies at will. The brilliant and the excellently prepared might choose wisely, but the majority would not. They would not because, in many areas, they have no experience which could make choice a reasonable endeavor. Choice without relevant experience is so unreal that it is closely akin to irrational chance. In the struggle of academic principles, one principle, that of entirely free electives, is wholly dead, apparently having no defenders. The students deserve some guidance, not only in the conduct of their studies, but in the determination of the kinds of studies they are to pursue.

The case against the elective system is strong and has been stated many times. One of the ablest statements of it is that provided by Professor Brand Blanshard, former head of the department of philosophy at Yale and before that at Swarthmore. Professor Blanshard's attack takes the form of questioning the premises on which an elective system rests. These are three, as follows: first, the premise "that the subjects and courses are of approximately equal value"; second, the notion that an education can be compounded out of "hours and credits"; and third, the idea "that the student is competent himself to fix the pattern of his education." [2] The very presentation of these premises is helpful in forwarding the entire discussion, for they are excellent examples of assumptions which are often unchallenged when they are not stated, but which are seen by all as fundamentally weak when once they are formulated.

The idea that subjects and courses are of equal value is part of the false democracy which endangers our culture. There is a profound level at which equality makes sense, but it does not often make sense at any other. Because professors are of vastly different

[2] Brand Blanshard, "Education as Philosophy," *Swarthmore College Bulletin*, Vol. XLII, No. 4, pp. 8, 9.

merit, their courses are bound to be unequal, even in the best colleges. To say that a course in ethics is equal in educational value to a course in badminton, just because they indicate the same number of hours of credit, is manifest nonsense. If graduation is accomplished by the mere process of adding hours, the student who combines a superficial cleverness with his laziness will find ways to make the addition less burdensome. Students soon learn which courses demand less work or are more likely to bring good grades. It is not possible to make a rational defense of a system which measures nothing but piecemeal achievements. What we must have, instead, is a meaningful plan, leading to an end, with some adequate means of judging total achievement.

The premise that the student is fully able to fix the pattern of his own education is the weakest of all. If a boy of eighteen comes to college, having just graduated from a high school in which the main enterprise was basketball, with no discernible intellectual discipline, what chance is there that he can have any intelligent judgment about his selection of studies? He may act like the child in the cafeteria line who loads up so heavily on sweets that there is no room for anything else. Apart from some literary experience, how does he know that *Wuthering Heights* is better reading than *Peyton Place*? How can he know the differences in value until the college has placed before him the best possible models of good thinking and good taste? Once he has come to have some firsthand acquaintance with the great models, he may be able to see for himself the shoddiness of the third- and fourth-rate achievements, but since this acquaintance is one of the main tasks of the college, it cannot be presumed in advance. If, as suggested earlier, the greatest of all sciences is the science of choice, the college has a responsibility to help each student to learn the rudiments of this science.

Eliminating the idea of complete and empty freedom, our live alternatives are really two. The first possibility is that of a common curriculum, once a recognized practice. There is something to be said for this, particularly in that it makes the degree of more uniform worth. If all students follow the same disciplines, and if we know what they are, we have a right to assume competence in these studies on the part of all graduates. But the evils of this system are so great as to make it wholly unsatisfactory. The chief evil is that it does not recognize the real differences between students in regard to interests and future hopes. It does not develop the power of rational choice. This leaves us with an alternative which involves neither a fully elective system nor a common curriculum, and to this third way we are driven by reason. The essence of the third way is a combination of limited electives, with increasing concentration on one field as the college career progresses, and a forced spread. The forced spread need not involve the assignment of particular courses, but does require that the student, during his college years and particularly during the early years, encounter a variety of studies. This has the double advantage of aiding in the development of a broader culture and in providing some solid experience in the light of which future choices can be intelligently made. It is not likely that a young man will elect to concentrate on the study of economics if he has never been introduced to the subject.

The conception of a forced spread of academic interest shows its soundness when it is combined with limited choice. A student may be required to submit to a full year's study of some social science because, as a chemist or physicist, he might otherwise neglect this field, but it is wise to permit him to choose, within the general field, among particular courses which satisfy the requirement. This avoids the foolishness of the cafeteria approach, but it also takes away the stigma of the one deeply hated required course. Always, one of our chief problems is motivation, and the lack of adequate incentive is much the most evident in the large required courses which students take only because they are forced to do so. The situation is not fair either to the instructor or the student and is sometimes so bad that a potentially noble subject is degraded by the process. Students can learn the art of choice by choosing early, within a limited range, and choosing later within a wider range. Thus every college career should involve a considerable width of choices, particularly at the end, but it should be so arranged that some minimum spread of interest can be assumed on the part of anyone who presents himself to the public as a graduate of the college. It is reasonable to require a minimum of two years' work in the natural sciences, two in the social sciences, and two in the humanities, including English language and literature. The unapologetically Christian college will normally require a certain minimum in religion and philosophy.

Quite as important as the right selection of subjects is the order in which studies occur. Because we care about our total culture we need to be clear about this, not merely in college, but throughout the educational effort. We have often supposed that the humanizing studies should come first and then the technical, but there is good psychological reason for reversing the process. The normal high school student has no real trouble in learning geometry, largely because geometry depends practically not at all on human experience. There is no good reason why plane geometry cannot be learned at twelve years of age, as Blaise Pascal did alone, almost as well as at twenty. But the notion that a person could profit by Aristotle's *Nicomachean Ethics* as much at twelve as at twenty is patently absurd. The sixteen-year-old, reading Milton's sonnet on his blindness, may miss, for the most part, the profound pathos and beauty of the lines; yet with four more years of experience and some firsthand knowledge of human tragedy, the same words may reach him at a deep place.

We should be wise if we were to concentrate in high school, not on social studies as we now do, but on mathematics and grammar, leaving politics and ethics and social theory to a period when these studies, though not fully understood even then, may at least be somewhat comprehensible. Here the wise words of Professor Barker demand serious attention.

The study of politics is beyond the capacity, or rather, beyond the range of experience, of the school boy. . . . It requires some previous experience of life. Before you can really study the theory of good and evil in ethics, you must have realized, in your own life, the existence of moral problems. Similarly before you can really study the theory of right and wrong in politics, you must have undergone some sort of political experience . . . you must have wrestled yourself, in some way, with the problems of conduct and organization which arise in human societies.[3]

Few advances in educational philosophy and educational practice would be as significant as a better division of academic labor between high school and college. Now the two tasks are so mixed that high schools try to do what ought to be reserved for college, with the result that colleges are forced to give high school training in basic technical subjects such as grammar, composition, and mathematics. The sensible division is made when the schools seek to provide training in those subjects which require less maturity, providing thereby materials on which later studies can be based, while the colleges teach those studies which require more maturity. No scholar in our time has been more clear on the nature of order in learning than Sir Richard Livingstone, particularly in the following sentences:

First note again that certain subjects need no experience of life for their full comprehension; among these are mathematics, languages, the sciences and some aspects of geography. No experience is required for such subjects. French or Latin, algebra or geometry, chemistry or physics, are perfectly intelligible, even if we have seen nothing of life or of men. They are like predigested foods, complete in themselves.[4]

What a joy it might be to teach in college if the students, when they come, could be assumed already to know elementary algebra, English grammar, and geography, and could really use some language other than their own. It would be far better to use time

[3] E. Barker, *The Citizen's Choice*, p. 150.
[4] Sir Richard Livingstone, *The Future in Education* (Cambridge, Eng.: Cambridge University Press, 1949), p. 19.

in high school developing such skills than in discussing the ethics of the New Deal or the race question, because these are subjects which require mature judgment for their comprehension. Much of our present confusion in education has arisen not because of the subjects we propose to teach, but because of a confusion in order. We shall not understand the idea of a college until we see where the college comes in a rational order. The ideal education may include elementary techniques at the beginning and advanced techniques at the end, with liberal arts and sciences in the middle. The college exists primarily to provide a community of academic life for this middle and crucial period.

The change of judgment that has come in our time in regard to what is called general education has been striking. Courses in general education, such as general physical science or general social science, were introduced with the laudable aim of widening the student's interest and knowledge. But a large number of these courses are now recognized as failures. The failures, as we analyze them, appear to come from the fact that the courses have been too generalized and too elementary. Often they have seemed to college students to be essentially repetitions of what was taught them in high school. The motivation is poor, partly because the most interesting parts of any study are never those which appear on the elementary level. A student's keen interest is more likely to be caught by a course in chemistry than by a course in general science. Similarly, he is more likely to be aroused to study in a course in philosophy than in a course in general humanities. Though requirements must be made, it is wise to help students into mature disciplines as rapidly as possible. Sometimes a boy develops almost unbreakable habits of laziness during his first two years of college because he never, in this time, is really challenged intellectually, but simply goes along, with hundreds of others, in the academic lockstep. Sometimes he starts with real enthusiasm, but finds this enthusiasm ebbing away because it takes too long to come to the studies which he really came to pursue. By the time he finally reaches these, he may be already ruined.

There is a valid place for generalization, but it comes better at the end of an undertaking than at the beginning. One can easily conceive of a brilliant effort at integration in social science on the part of seniors who have something to integrate, having already studied in strong courses in political science, sociology, and economics, as well as history. For years at Haverford College there was a required philosophy course, taught by the great Rufus Jones, but it was not for freshmen or sophomores; it was for seniors. Fortunately, the main intellectual current of our day is moving in the direction of strong and specific courses as early as possible. The question is never whether we favor general education, for everyone recognizes that we must avoid a too narrow education; the question is the level at which generalization is profitable. A course in general knowledge is a manifest absurdity. Furthermore, the most specific of studies, such as that of ancient Roman history, is always given wide reference by a good teacher. The good Latin teacher, in introducing high school students to the *Gallic Wars*, will naturally illuminate Caesar's gathering of boats for the invasion of Britain in 55 B.C. by reference to Hitler's abortive gathering on the same coast so many years later.

Integration, however badly the term has been mishandled, is certainly something to achieve. The way of wisdom is not to dismiss it because it has become part of an unlovely jargon but to try to see what its deeper significance may be. Real integration comes, not by the introduction of both chemistry and physics into a single course, or by any other such combination; it comes by the production of a cast of mind which can be employed in dealing with any subject. This is what we ordinarily mean by the philosophic mentality. The essence of it is the ability to explain by the effort to relate. Error arises by separation from context. To call man a mechanism is erroneous, not because there are not some mechanical features in a human body, but because such a simplification distorts the total picture by all that it omits. It leaves out purposes, it leaves out emotions, it leaves out meanings. We are hindered from knowing the total truth about anything because, in our inevitable finitude, we never see all of the relations of any fact to other facts, but our responsibility is to see and appreciate as much relatedness as can be grasped by creatures like ourselves. It is especially important for us to learn that it is never good enough to embrace a proposition if we are not also willing to embrace all of the implications of that proposition which are known to us to follow. In practically every case the opponents of Socrates, in the dialogues, failed at this point. They wanted to accept propositions without their consequences. What Socrates was teaching mankind was integration at a level of intellectual and moral depth. We have made a brave start on the integration of modern education when we have taught our students to follow the argument where it leads, whatever the particular subject.

A college would be on the road to success if it were to try to arrange things so that the finest and most exciting teachers would teach the freshmen. Almost anyone can teach advanced students without significant harm. What goes on in the early part of a college career ought to be the kind of instruction which raises, with urgency, a host of problems which the student can use the rest of his time in trying, with the help of books and professors, and by his own developing thought, to answer. The best questions will usually be aroused most insistently by contacts with the best minds. That is why the finest beginning, in the study of philosophy, is not some modern textbook, but the dialogues of Plato. By plunging into these at once, in depth, the ordinary student soon discovers in himself both unknown questions and unknown intellectual powers. Even more important, the callow student, as he digs into the dialogues, may begin to recognize his own ignorance and thus, as Socrates said, make a remarkable advance. Plato taught all the world to recognize how easily men can be wrong, even in their most cherished opinions. The student who begins with Plato is involved, from the start, with a marvelous combination, as seen in the person of Socrates, of both humility and greatness. If he understands anything of the teaching in regard to the recognition of error as the precondition of all search for truth, he is bound to apply it to his own life.

Compare this beginning with that in which the student is started with a textbook, which, in the effort to explain, is more likely to succeed only in making the subject seem dull and prosaic. Even the beginning student can sense the difference in value between the *Symposium* and such a contemporary production, which may be utterly forgotten in ten years. He understands President Hollinshead, formerly of Coe College, who describes a textbook as a book which, "in the dullest language imaginable," tries "to summarize the thought of several men, each greater than the compiler." [5]

There are some courses in which the use of a textbook is wise or even necessary, but there is no doubt that the current use of these devices is terribly overdone. We need textbooks in logic and in certain courses in mathematics and perhaps in elementary language, such as beginning Greek, but there are other courses in which textbooks are introduced as a kind of convention and apparently without serious consideration of alternatives. Why, for example, have a textbook in ethics? The use of a textbook tends, in such a course, to be a limiting rather than a liberating factor, giving too much emphasis to one contemporary system which is likely to be of only temporary significance in human thought. It is far better for the course to be free-ranging, the students reading Aristotle and Kant and a dozen more whose giant minds are not on trial. In such a course, if our aim is intellectual maturity, the place of the textbook is on some library shelf, while the books in the hands of the students should be some acknowledged classics. With the abundance of inexpensive reprints now available in nearly all fields of thought, there is no longer any excuse for the adoption of the bulky books which students in most colleges today carry from class to class. We need to realize that the textbook is far more suitable to high

[5] Byron S. Hollinshead, "The Curriculum of Phantom College," *School and Society*, Vol. 69, No. 1779, pp. 65–69.

school than to college age. The liberation from the textbook is one
of our chief ways of raising our academic sights and overcoming the
artificial extension of intellectual adolescence. Even when a textbook is needed, it should be minimized and made merely a starting
point for the really mature work of the course. We give our case
away when we refer to "outside reading." Outside of what? Why
not just "reading"? Sometimes we even reveal the mood of intellectual infantilism by speaking of "homework." The term is
particularly inane when the students live in the college and presumably do their work there.

A great part of a rational curriculum is the reading of books.
Consequently the instruction must be so arranged that students
develop, first, a desire to read; second, some understanding of what
to read; and, finally, some judgment of their own regarding the
value of different books. This process can be expedited, if we will,
by earlier introduction to what is truly excellent and has been
judged so by the best minds of different generations. Herein lies
the positive strength of the Great Books movement. It is a mistake
to build a curriculum about the progressive reading of classics,
chiefly because in the natural sciences there are no classics in the
sense that they exist in religion and poetry. Science, by its nature,
is a cumulative discipline in which the latest efforts are the ones to
note because they combine what is best in former efforts. The
student of the natural sciences may read Galen and Newton for
historic interest, but if he wants to advance, he ought to get into
the laboratory and go forward with the help of the latest theories
and instruments. With true classics, however, the situation is
intrinsically different because these are independent of a cumulative process. Milton's sonnet "On His Blindness" is not affected
one way or another by changing conceptions of the science of optics.
The difference is well demonstrated in our present relationship
to Blaise Pascal. Though his scientific achievements are great, there
is little reason for studying them now, and the physics student is
well advised to deal with contemporary physics, but the situation

is radically different in regard to the *Pensées* or *The Provincial Letters*. Pascal's deepest thoughts on the deepest subjects thrill all but the dullest students and seem to be dateless. Almost any student can rightly complain later that he has been cheated if he is not introduced at some point to stimulation of this character.

There is no hard-and-fast rule about the point in a student's development when he should encounter different subjects. This is why we need wise teachers, watching, advising, and checking. The task of advising cannot be left to a professional class called advisers or counselors with no teaching duties. The best adviser is the instructor himself, especially if he has broken through the student's guard and caught his interest. The second Oliver Wendell Holmes was a fortunate young man when at Harvard he had advice of this kind both within the college and outside. One day, when Professor George Martin Lane guessed that young Holmes was ready, he handed him a book, saying, "This was written yesterday. It will be your exciting privilege to discover a new writer." The book was the *Republic*. Holmes devoted his six weeks' winter vacation to reading the book and wrote a fifteen-page paper in which, with youthful self-assurance, he attempted to criticize the book harshly. Being wise enough already, however, to seek corroboration or help, he showed his paper to Ralph Waldo Emerson, his father's friend. Emerson read the paper carefully, shook his head, and uttered just one sentence, "When you shoot at a king you must kill him." Holmes got the point and flung his paper into the wastebasket. He had received timely help from two wise men.

We cannot expect every college student to be as fortunate in his counselors as Holmes was, but this is the ideal at which we point. The wise professor will not only hand out books when the students are ready to receive them; he will also advise about new studies, including those outside his own department. When Herbert Hoover was a freshman at Stanford, he already knew that he wanted to be a geological engineer, and went early to the head of the geology department for counsel. It was this geologist who advised him to spend some time on the other side of the inner quadrangle with Professor Murray in the study of classics, partly because contact with Augustus Murray was sure to be broadening. Young Hoover took the advice, with several concrete results. One was that, years later, Mr. and Mrs. Hoover translated a Latin work, and the other was that Professor Murray became the lifelong friend of the Hoovers, going with them to Washington, when Hoover became President, to give whatever help he could.

The wise teacher will try to know when to hand to the student the new book, not too soon and not too late. This takes a skill so great that no person feels adequate in practicing it. When, for example, is the right time to start a young person on poetry? Those who have read Virginia Woolf's wise essay "How Should One Read a Book?" will not be likely to forget her answer to this question. The time to read poetry, she said, is "when we are almost able to write it." No person can appreciate poetry unless he is already something of a poet in his heart. There is inexhaustible loveliness in the lines

> The moving Moon went up the sky,
> And nowhere did abide;
> Softly she was going up,
> And a star or two beside.

but the loveliness is hidden from the person who is not ready. Sometimes the young person becomes ready with amazing speed, in a few days. The teacher who cares will watch for these crucial days, knowing that a great part of the art of teaching consists in the perception of readiness.

One hindrance to the development of intellectual maturity in our colleges is the existence of too many offerings. Most students take too many courses, touching all of them superficially and trying too many at the same time. The most common undergraduate pattern in America today demands five courses in a semester, each with three hours credit. The continuance of this for eight semesters gives credit for 120 hours, the number often required for a bachelor's degree. However deeply imbedded in our culture this pattern is, it is wrong and it is wrong because it introduces the student to too much scattering of interest. We should progress better and faster if we were to limit each student to four or even three courses at a time and seek to make each more demanding. It is not necessary to go so far in the other direction as to have only one course at a time. A little variety is stimulating, but too much is enfeebling.

Such a system of fewer courses will mean that a student will not be able to have all of the courses he needs in four years. The answer to this is that knowledge of a subject is not dependent on having a course in it. There is no justification whatever for an advanced student to excuse his ignorance of something on the ground that he never took a course in it. The purpose of a course is not to teach everybody everything, but to give students such a start and such incentive that they can go forward for themselves. We practice too much the holding the student's hand instead of allowing him as he advances to become responsible for his own life. This growth in responsibility is involved in the entire philosophy of limited electives, with growing experience of choice.

Part of the disgrace of modern colleges is that there is too much attendance at classes and not enough learning. Often, we bring something to a boy's attention when we have reason to believe that he is ready, but he is so occupied with class attendance and trivial busy work that he claims to have no time for the great opportunity. We should simplify the schedule so that the student can have large blocks of time for mature, independent work. There will be some who are unable to take good advantage of this, but this is the price we shall have to pay for excellence. Certainly we cannot expect a student to accomplish mature work if he is always walking back and forth to classes.

The idea of independent study under affectionate guidance is so good that carefully selected students, in their third or fourth years, may reasonably be freed from all classwork in order to accomplish something of first-rate value. Some of this has already been tried, with remarkable success. There are some risks in this method, but the potential results are so good that the risks are worth taking. What is important to realize is that the risks of the alternative system are also great and even greater. Any curriculum is a success if it is infused with the intelligent purpose of recognizing and producing a greater responsibility and maturity in student life.

VII

Liberal and Vocational Education

"I call therefore a complete and generous education that which fits a man to perform justly, skilfully, and magnanimously all the offices both private and public, of peace and war."

JOHN MILTON

THOUGH there are many useful ways of classifying institutions of higher learning, the classification which is most familiar to contemporary citizens is that of liberal and vocational education. The former has already been outlined, in part, in the preceding chapter, but it is not what thousands of parents have in mind when they consider the further education, beyond high school, of their children, and particularly of their sons. What many have in mind is the reasonably simple notion of getting a young man ready to be an engineer. The fact that the Russians now graduate annually more engineers than we do has accentuated our purpose in this familiar direction. Millions, when they think of college, think primarily of one thing—how can the student be prepared most perfectly or most quickly to do the work associated with his intended vocation or profession? Why not, many ask, proceed at once to the serious business of technology, which is the distinguishing mark of our age, leaving out all the decorations and fancy courses that are a waste of time? Get on with your chemistry, learn to use the slide rule, get

95

through college and get on with the job, is advice that makes sense to a great many people. More and more, because of the way in which the issues of competitive coexistence present themselves, this is the simple form which educational philosophy will take.

As we try to consider the value of a purely vocational education, we are wise to begin with its strengths. The major strength of all higher education which is deliberately and directly pointed toward competence in a particular job is that it solves, in large measure, the problem of incentive. However noble may be the purpose of our big required courses in "Contemporary Civilization," the sober truth is that a large proportion of the students resist full participation in them and accordingly function at a low intellectual level, primarily because they see no practical utility in what they are doing. What does the reading of Dante have to do with my work as my father's successor as manager of the chain of grocery stores? There is an answer to this question and it is often given, but the sad fact is that the nineteen-year-old does not really hear it. Consequently he goes on looking out the window, waiting for the bell to ring and the hour to end.

This problem hardly ever arises in the educational work that is frankly vocational. There is no problem about incentive in a medical school, and this for several reasons. One reason is that entrance is peculiarly difficult and that all students are aware of the fact that others would like to occupy their places. Another is that each medical student wants desperately to be a successful physician, and he can see that if this end is to be accomplished, he must learn all that he can about anatomy and surgery and medicine. Each item bears with terrible urgency upon his future practice. The study provides its own incentive because it is eminently practical.

We have seen earlier that if we do not solve the problem of incentive, much that we do is a failure, and now we see that vocational education provides a way of solving this problem. It has been the custom of many academicians in recent years to look with some contempt upon mere professional education, an institution so organ-

ized being dubbed a "barber college," but it is time now to reconsider our judgment. At least the technical institute is not a
kindergarten for grown children; at least it is not a country club
where the children of the reasonably well-to-do put off, for four
years, the evil day when they have to go to work; at least it is not
an institution dedicated primarily to the achievement of social
prestige.

The great sources of incentive in human life are ultimately four.
In the first place men will work for more *money*. This is not despised
by any thoughtful person, because money will get several other
things that men desire, including assistance to others. We are bound
to admire the earthy common sense of Dr. Johnson to the effect that
there is nothing demeaning about writing for money, and we can
apply the same standard to a host of other pursuits. That money is
a needed incentive even the Communists have been forced to admit, as they have altered their system of rewards. The second major
incentive is *recognition*. Men work for honor, including reputation
in the years after they are gone from the earthly scene. This, too,
is not to be neglected, for it is one of the facts of life. A third source
of incentive is satisfaction in *achievement*. Man is so made that he
rejoices in the sense of a job well done. Aristotle was so impressed
with this aspect of human life that he considered production, especially the production of excellence, as the greatest occasion for human happiness. In the fourth place, many men work to promote
some *cause* to which they are committed, with little or no reference
to their own self-interests. Fortunately these four ends are not incompatible with one another, but can profitably be combined.

In a college, there is not much place for the financial motive,
though money prizes are honorable. Lord Tweedsmuir has told us
in *Pilgrim's Way* how he, a poor boy, made his way through college
almost wholly on prize money, and in view of his magnificent use of
his education we cannot but be glad that such prizes were available.
Students may also be aware of future financial prizes if they do
good work and graduate, but much of the power of this argument

has now been lost. It was once the fashion to point out that high school graduates could expect, on the average, to earn a certain amount, and that college graduates could expect to earn more, but this is now out of date. Many of those with the largest incomes are uninfluenced by higher education of any kind, while, on the other hand, many college graduates earn less than they might, not because they do not value money, but because they value something else more. Doctors and engineers, it is true, are likely to earn more than the average citizen, but the same is not true of teachers, and none of them will earn as much as a really successful salesman, who may have only an elementary education.

The second major incentive, honor, can have a considerable bearing on educational life and ought to have. It makes a difference whether a man merely graduates or graduates with distinction. Election to student offices, far from being something to be minimized, is an excellent indication of leadership and a good preparation for participation in a free society. If we were wise we should find ways of giving as much honor, within a college, to scholarly achievement as to that which comes from participation in an athletic program.

Important as these two sources of incentive are, it is the third and fourth that are the greatest and most enduring. The head of a company may have ceased, long ago, to work primarily for money because he has a sufficiency, and he may have all the honors he seeks, but he continues his hard work and long hours because of the motive of achievement or because he cares. Sometimes a manager wants to see the business straightened out, to overcome obstacles to smooth operation, to make a difference and a permanent difference while he lives. Vocational education ties in with this motive easily and obviously, and this is its major advantage. What we must do is to go on and try to make the student see that full achievement requires far more than mere technical competence. Above all, we must teach the nobility of commitment.

It may be hard for the engineering student to know it in his undergraduate days, but full achievement will require far more than knowledge of the principles and practices of engineering. The head of a great engineering firm feels fortunate about his education because he took the basic engineering courses in his freshman year and after that made economics his field of concentration. Part of the reason for his present outstanding success, he believes, arises from the fact that he became interested in something *besides* engineering. The truth is that a man may learn to use a slide rule and still be a stupid boor. If he knows engineering and nothing else, if he has no social concern, if his aim is mere technical competence and the financial rewards of that competence, such as a late-model car and a home in the suburbs, he may not in reality be an educated man at all. The exact problem which he deals with in his technical college will seldom be met in practical life. He may find that his chief problems are personal, particularly those involved in getting along with other workers. Often his greatest need is judgment, but it is clear that skill in judgment does not come by attendance in a particular course.

The central point to keep in mind is that a person is not merely an engineer or a lawyer, but primarily a *man*. In the long run the kind of technician a person is depends upon the kind of man he is. The purpose of an educational system, as John Stuart Mill said in his inaugural address as rector of St. Andrews University, is to make "capable and cultivated human beings. Men are men before they are lawyers or physicians or manufacturers; and if you make them capable and sensible men, they will make themselves capable and sensible lawyers or physicians." The motive of practical achievement is sound and trustworthy, but the task of educators is to enlarge students' conceptions of what adequate or self-justifying achievement may be. Our task is not to neglect the powerful incentive of vocational education, but to enlarge it. In this effort Justice Frankfurter, writing to a young man who inquired of him regarding the best preparation for the practice of law, has helped all who will listen:

The best way to prepare for the law is to come to the study of the law as a well-read person. Thus alone can one acquire the capacity to use the English language on paper and in speech and with the habits of clear thinking which only a true liberal education can give. *No less important for a lawyer is the cultivation of the imaginative faculties by reading poetry, seeing great paintings, in the original or in easily available reproductions, and listening to great music.* Stock your mind with the deposit of much good reading, and widen and deepen your feelings by experiencing vicariously as much as possible the wonderful mysteries of the universe, and forget all about your future career.

A great number of those now in college, particularly the young men, will become businessmen, and this is as it should be. We cannot keep up our society without them. We need persons who buy and sell and distribute both goods and services. But what is the best training for these persons? There may be helpful courses in business management, but most of this will, in any case, be learned on the job. What the businessman needs for practical purposes is ease and clarity of communication. He must know how to speak and how to write, both of which are skills which can be learned. Indeed, he is not likely to develop these skills unless they are specifically taught. People can learn, under competent guidance, ways of expression and of notation that are superior to other ways. We have only to compare the clumsy Roman system of numeration with the Arabic to see what a vast difference a superior language can make.

The businessman ought to be a leader of thought and opinion in his own community, but he is not likely to be a good leader if he has not learned to think. In this an encounter with Aristotle may help him immensely all of his life. He may, as a consequence, learn to detect fallacies and to pierce through the sophistry of specious reasoning. The prospective businessman can be helped greatly by visits to the college of men who are successful in their chosen callings and know something besides their particular work. Such men can tell the young what they are glad they studied and what they wish they had studied.

Far from omitting reference to vocations, we ought to expect some vocational competence on the part of all who teach. Perhaps the student is justified in refusing to pay attention to some old fuddy-duddy who is rightly suspected of taking up teaching because he could not succeed in any ordinary pursuit. The speech teacher ought to be able to demonstrate as well as to advise; in short, he should, first of all, be a speaker. The one who teaches teachers ought to have taught, and have taught successfully. The one who teaches home economics ought to have had a home, and the one who talks about family life ought to have had a family.

Having said all this, and recognizing the real strength in vocational education, we are in a position to try to evaluate the education that is generally known as liberal. By liberal studies we mean those which are pursued without any immediate or obvious utilitarian purpose. Professional studies need no defense because everyone sees that we must have them if our social order is to continue. But liberal studies do need a defense, for there are many who think of them as outmoded or irrelevant. Do we any longer have time, it is seriously asked, for the frosting on the cake?

Part of the danger of the sense of urgency which is the public reaction to Soviet superiority in some fields of technology, and specifically in ballistics, is that we may be tempted to give up the whole idea of the American college. What many are actually asking for is the introduction of the European conception in which students go straight from secondary school training to a university in which the courses are mainly utilitarian. Even the European boy who studies Greek at the university level studies it professionally. The characteristic European student is thereby denied much that our development of the college system has made possible. Ordinarily he does not learn any philosophy unless he expects to be a professional philosopher. That this is a severe loss there is no serious doubt. But voices are now raised to declare that we can no longer afford the luxury of studying something which will not have immediate utilitarian value. Since we are in a time of crisis, many raise the question whether we ought to spend any energy on what has no utility.

Many references in the current educational debate have been

made to the quotable remarks of Professor George Boas of Johns
Hopkins University before a Chicago meeting of the Association
for Higher Education. His words gain extra importance in the light
of the fact that they were uttered more than six years before the
appearance of the first sputnik. Part of what Professor Boas said
was:

We are in a national situation where millions are being spent daily
on studies the results of which will be weapons. The more deadly
the weapons, the better. Pure science is tolerated because it is suspected that it may contain implications useful for warfare. Psychology
and economics are permitted because it is hoped that the former may
teach us how to beguile the enemy into treason or cowardice, the
latter because it may teach us how to capture or destroy the materials
vital to the enemy's defense. But the historian, the student of language and literature, and especially that human gadfly the philosopher, are not encouraged. They are not essential to defense. They
are merely essential to civilization.[1]

It is the last two sentences which have been quoted most frequently,
apparently because they made a point which others felt dimly,
but could not say so well.

Before we can answer with any adequacy the question regarding
utility in education, we must consider critically the whole notion
of *use*, for the idea is far from being as simple as it appears to be.
That is useful which gives human beings what they need. They
need food and clothing and security, but these are certainly not all
that we need. Our most insistent need is to learn to live. That
study, therefore, has the greatest potential utility which may reasonably be expected to help men to *be* and not merely to *have*.
What we require, first of all, is something to help us to live with
ourselves. Plato makes Socrates say, in dealing with this question,
that the permanently best saying is to the effect that "the useful
is the noble." [2] Most of what we normally call useful is merely
some step on the way to what is intrinsically valuable and there-

[1] The address was printed in the *Journal of Higher Education*, May 1951.
[2] *Republic*, Book V, 457 b.

fore useful in the terminal sense. We rightly think of radiant health as such a good in itself, for it is worth having, even though it leads to nothing beyond itself. It is, accordingly, worth seeking and cherishing. The same can be said, on a higher level, of a cultivated mind. "I say," says Newman, "that a cultivated intellect, because it is a good in itself, brings with it a power and a grace to every work and occupation which it undertakes, and enables us to be more useful, and to a greater number." [3] The paradox is that our greatest good to society often comes, not by any intention to develop a utilitarian skill, but by concentration on that which is good in its own right.

All of us have a social responsibility, but we are not likely to be of any real help to other people unless we have something of value within our own lives. The urge to participate in service organizations is often sheer sentimentality, because the individual so urged is seldom encouraged to examine his own life to see what he has to offer. The very notion that we are, by nature, the givers and the others the receivers is repulsive once it is rationally examined. The blind, we are told on the best authority, cannot lead the blind. Thoreau provided a sharp reminder of this essential human situation in the motto over the door of his hut: "My destiny mended here, not yours." A liberal education may provide the best antidote to naïve altruism in that it encourages us to have something worth giving before we start to give. A liberal education is sure to bring us into contact with the really great minds and, though this does not always prove effective, it may induce the beneficent humility which leads, not merely to service, but to mutual assistance in the great business of living.

Marten Ten Hoor has put many scholars in his debt by his brilliant essay "Education for Privacy." In this he starts with the principle that the only way to improve society is to improve oneself and suggests that "a major in the social sciences does not automat-

[3] John Henry Newman, *The Idea of a University* (London: Longmans, Green & Company, 1929), p. 167.

ically qualify a student for social leadership." We have, he says, to live well with ourselves before we can live well with others. But millions in the modern world resist aloneness. If a person is alone in a room, he often turns on the radio and suffers its frequent inanity because this is an alternative to the silence which he so hates and fears. He hates the silence because he does not have the inner resources for meditation that can make silence glorious. The sad fact is that this occurs in many lives which have supposedly been exposed to an education. The Gallup poll shows that though the expenditure for education has increased, the proportion of adults who read books is steadily decreasing. It has gone down in twenty years from 29 per cent to only 17 per cent. A really liberal education, if successful in reaching the students, would change this and this consideration alone would be a sufficient justification. One test of a liberal education is appreciation of such a paragraph as the following:

Let us consider one form of art enjoyment which is available to virtually every normal human being, young or old, learned or simple, saint or sinner—reading. Its great virtue for education for privacy is that it is a strictly private experience. No other human being is necessary to the reader at the moment of reading. He can take his book with him to the jungle or the desert, on the ocean or the mountain top. He can select his company at will, and rid himself of it by a turn of the hand. It is potentially an inexhaustible resource: all ages of history; all countries; all varieties of human beings, and even of animals and plants and physical things; the entire range of human thoughts and feelings, hopes and fears, conquests and failures, victories and defeats; the real and the ideal—all are available at the turn of a page for the reader's contemplation and understanding.[4]

Unfortunately there are college graduates who admit, or even boast, that they have read no books at all since leaving college. Their education was a waste of their time and of those who strove to teach them. But this is precisely what we must try, with all the intelligence we can muster, to change. A liberal education can help

[4] Marten Ten Hoor, "Education for Privacy," *The American Scholar*, Vol. 23, No. 1.

men and women to live better both with themselves and with others. It does this in many ways, but three are paramount. In the first place, it tends to encourage the development of intellectual discipline. The heart of this discipline is the habit of always asking for the evidence. All who engage in a liberal education are, in some sense or other, students of Socrates, and this is the question he taught men to ask. The person who is liberally trained will ask it, not only about bridges or medicine, but about propositions of every kind on every subject. In religion, he will not rest content with uncritical faith or with uncritical rejection, but will proceed to inquire, using the same intellectual tools in this field that he would use with a problem in atomic physics. He will do the same in regard to comments about men and movements. If he hears a political leader maligned, he will naturally ask, "How do you know? What is the evidence? Is this merely hearsay?"

We are not likely to improve on Newman's account of the value of intellectual discipline. "We know," he wrote, "not by a direct and simple vision, not at a glance, but, as it were, by piecemeal and accumulation, by a mental process, by going round an object, by the comparison, the combination, the mutual correction, the continual adaptation, of many partial notions, by the joint application and concentration upon it of many faculties and exercises of mind. Such a union and concert of the intellectual powers, such an enlargement and development, such a comprehensiveness, is necessarily a matter of training. And, again, such a training is a matter of rule. . . . The eye of the mind, of which the object is truth, is the work of discipline and habit." [5]

What is sad about some kinds of education is not that they fail to impart a knowledge of specific and isolated facts, but that they teach men to be critical in only one area. Thus it is not uncommon for a man to be an excellent scientist, in a restricted field, and yet not be in the least bothered about the fact that he is using his skill and knowledge to help support a totalitarian regime. In

[5] Newman, *The Idea of a University*, p. 151.

contemporary Russia we see a widespread and alarming example of this tendency, and it is still the dominant one, even though we may have eventual hope of the effect of liberal ideas. On a smaller scale such academic provincialism was illustrated among the men who served Adolf Hitler. Not all of those who have experienced liberal studies are free from this evil, but, as we go from college to college, we can easily see that more of them are free from it than can be found in a narrowly technical training. For the most part, the frightening thing about those who are students of technology and nothing else is their terrible naïveté on moral and social questions. They have a discipline, but it is not large enough. The first purpose of a liberal education is to extend the area of human inquiry.

The second way in which a liberal education becomes truly and fundamentally useful is that it aids in the development of an educated taste. Human beings of every level of civilization and intelligence are always making judgments of taste, revealing thereby what they think is beautiful or excellent or vulgar or ugly or worthless. Now it is obvious, not only that human taste differs enormously, but that some judgments are far sounder than others. At some points of intellectual immaturity it is fashionable to say that tastes cannot be argued and that one aesthetic judgment is therefore as good as another. Apparently, however, nobody actually believes this, for the very persons who say it proceed to argue vehemently. There may be people in London who think the St. Pancras Railway Station is more beautiful than the Church of St. Clement Danes, but, if so, they are simply wrong. Appreciation can change, just as knowledge can change, and it is a great part of the purpose of education to help it to change in an intelligent and mature direction. Professor Blanshard has put the point vividly by saying, "It is natural that a boy of eight should regard Joe Palooka as the creation of genius; if he holds this opinion at eighteen, he is suffering from arrested development; if he holds it at fifty-eight, he is suffering from premature senility." [6]

[6] Brand Blanchard, *The Uses of a Liberal Education* (The Hazen Pamphlets, No. 26), pp. 15, 16.

Education is, in part, the process of learning to like the right things. This is a field in which we can be greatly helped by those farther along the road. The young man of twenty might not, by himself, enjoy *Sartor Resartus* at all, or might pronounce it dull; but with the help of a great teacher like Bliss Perry, he is likely both to understand it and to enjoy it. Judgment of others is always, in part, a self-judgment. Young Holmes's judgment of Plato was really a judgment of his own immaturity, but the remarkable thing was that he recognized that this was the case when Emerson pointed it out to him so laconically. The story of Whistler and his unappreciative critic has been told many times, but it bears repetition because it states the situation perfectly. "Mr. Whistler," said a lady to whom the painter had shown one of his pictures, "I never saw a sunset like that." To which he answered, "Madam, don't you wish you could?"

There is no simple and easy way to grow in taste, but some conditions are more productive of growth than others. The best condition known is that of a college in which people who care help one another to *grow*. The truth is that many things are invisible until we see them through others' eyes. This is, in great measure, the purpose of a college. A college exists to help people to have delights which otherwise they would, in all probability, have missed. As we read T. S. Eliot today we surmise that one of the best products of his liberal education was the ability to take joy in reading Lancelot Andrewes. What we need to remember is that this is an advanced taste and would not be likely to come to a man alone. In no area is the necessity of the community of search more evident than in this one.

A college is a community so planned that, through its creative fellowship, judgment is improved. In Newman's great words, it "aims at raising the intellectual tone of society, at cultivating the public mind, at purifying the national taste, at supplying true principles to popular enthusiasm and fixed aims to popular aspiration, at giving enlargement and sobriety to the ideas of the age, at facilitating the exercise of political power, and refining the intercourse of private life." [7] Not all of those who engage in a liberal education develop an educated taste, but the probability that they will be able to develop it in any other way is slight.

The third and greatest use of a liberal education is that it can help a person to discover a pattern of meaning which will give potential dignity to the separated aspects of his experience. Nobody is more miserable than the person who merely performs a task and does not know why. Men can endure great hardship for a reason, but what they cannot permanently endure is a sense of meaninglessness. A man who faces a liberal education with humility has an excellent chance of finding a meaning for his own little life because he has found meaning in the world. As he matches his mind with the best minds that have ever been, he may begin to see dimly one great story, of which his own career may be a small part, the story of the struggle of civilization in spite of wanton cruelty and sin and stupidity. He will come to see the essential similarity of the human situation in different ages of history and will understand that human nature is not greatly altered by the possession of machines. He will realize that men of an earlier day were worthy of his attention even though they were never able to travel faster than a horse could run. He will not, therefore, be contemptuous of what is not contemporary.

Some of those who share in a liberal education will have the enormous advantage of being able to profit from the Biblical insights into the meaning of human life and will, thereby, be able to envisage a pattern more clearly. Such may see a thread of purpose in creation, namely, that the creation is to be "set free from its bondage to decay and obtain the glorious liberty of the children of God" (Romans 8:21). Because the student who senses some of the profundity of this idea will understand that the world is in turmoil, "groaning in travail together until now," he will never be the victim of an easy optimism, but neither will he be the victim of an easy pessimism, for he will see the ultimate end as *redemp-*

[7] *The Idea of a University*, pp. 177, 178.

tion. Furthermore, he will be convinced that in all this we do not toil alone, for he will be persuaded that "in everything God works for good with those who love Him."

Not all, of course, who share in liberal studies will come to accept this particular pattern, even when the college of liberal studies is a Christian college; but in order to live well, each individual must find some pattern which makes sense. Men cannot live well unless they have something to live *for*. We cannot legislate in advance what this is, but we can provide the setting and the opportunity which enable the student to find it for himself. Education is a failure unless it turns the potential dignity of every individual into the actual dignity, which depends, chiefly, upon the recognition by each one of his own true vocation.

Thus, in the end, the conceptions of liberal and vocational education really come together. Vocation is a great word, with a freight of meaning. It involves the notion that each person is needed in the achievement of the total purpose. Historically the word has meant a great deal more than a reference to an occupation. The basic call is something of surpassing dignity, the call to a covenant relation between God and man. Professor Robert L. Calhoun of Yale, who has thought long and productively on this theme, states the central point with vividness. "In the long history of the Jewish and Christian churches," he says concerning vocation, "the term has a far more deep-cutting and momentous significance" than that of daily task. "It means God's summons, God's call, God's word addressed to a whole people, and to every individual member of that people. Vocation is God's word of command and word of promise." [8] There is nothing wrong with the idea of vocational education, especially when the notion of calling is retained in its full glory. Work is noble, especially when a man is seeking to be to God what a man's own hand is to a man. The reasonable effect of a truly liberal and generous education is not to make men contemptuous

[8] Robert L. Calhoun, "Christian Vocation on the College Campus," *The Christian Scholar*, Vol. XXXVII, Autumn 1954, p. 275.

of vocational training, but to dignify it by making it part of a larger whole.

Both vocational and liberal education are harmed by being envisaged in separation. The one alone produces men who are ignorant though narrowly skilled, while the other alone tends to produce a superficial cultivation without real drive. As soon as we realize that we are trying to produce whole persons, we know that the two chief forms of education are needed together.[9] One-sided education is always poor education. The lives of whole men must include both worship and work, both discipline and freedom, both respect for the individual and concern for the group, both the training of the mind and the training of the body, both cultural breadth and vocational competence.

The ideal education involves, at the same time, the powerful incentive which preparation for employment provides, and the breadth of view which humanizing studies can provide. The task is to combine them in such a way that both advantages are retained. Instead of being something new, this is our great tradition. Our first college was frankly vocational, though it was more than that. The well-known words at the west gate of Harvard make this clear:

After God had carried us safe to New England and wee had builded our houses provided necessaries for our liveli-hood reard convenient places for Gods worship and setled the Civill Government: One of the next things wee longed for and looked after was to advance Learning and perpetuate it to Posterity dreading to leave an illiterate Ministery to the Churches when our present ministers shall lie in the Dust.

The best education is that of the person who knows what he wants to do and accordingly moves forward with his own self-starter, but is helped to see the wider realms of thought, beyond his area of professional competence, which will help him to be both a better

[9] Thus Woodrow Wilson: "The liberal education that our professional men get must not only be antecedent to their technical training; it must also be concurrent with it." *Op. cit.*, p. 230.

worker and a better man. But what about the young person who does not know where he is going? Thousands start to college with no clear ideas of ultimate employment or profession, and thousands more change their plans two or three times in the course of college life. What is important to say is that this is not a calamity. Sometimes, if a man is really searching, it is better to search longer and more carefully. To the young man who does not know his life work we can say, "Relax. Use your college experience to *find* your way."

Decision regarding occupation is a serious one, often determining where a person lives and the level at which he lives. It is almost as important as marriage. Because it is so important, much of college life should be pointed toward the process of intelligent discovery. This can be done in many ways, but the best is by unhurried discussion between the students and the older teachers whom they have reason to respect. The older man may help the younger man to see that, important as a vocational decision is, the decision about the kind of person he is to be is far more important. As a matter of fact, a really gifted man would undoubtedly succeed in a number of different lines of work. An able man may even elect, as Lord Tweedsmuir did, to live his life in chapters and thus perform more than one kind of work. What is more important than the work is the creative habit of mind which a person brings to any task. It would be hard to surpass the ancient wisdom to the effect that if the general judgment is right, the details can be handled as they come. "If our citizens are well educated and grow into sensible men," said Socrates, "they will easily see their way through all these, as well as other matters which I omit." [10]

[10] *Republic*, IV, 423 e.

VIII

The Education of Men and Women

"When you educate a man, you educate an individual; when you educate a woman, you educate a family."

MARY LYON

THE college, like all other human institutions, must reckon with the fact that the world has both men and women in it. Consequently it is necessary to try to discover how a college education can be rightly related to differences of sex. Should we say, as once we did say, that a college education should be reserved for those of the male sex? If we reject this answer as an outworn and unjustified conception, recognizing our duty to include women as well as men in higher education, how shall the combination be handled? Should they be taught together? Should they live in the same academic community? Should they engage in the same intellectual disciplines? Should young men and young women ordinarily spend the same number of years in college? These and many other questions demand answers if we are seeking to learn not merely what has been but what ought to be.

Insofar as the western world is concerned, the battle for equality of opportunity for both sexes has been won. Seventy-five years ago it was an open question, with much argument on both sides and some bitterness, but most of the discussion is now outmoded. The militant feminism which was the creed of many of those who fought for women's education seems quite as quaint as does the argument against the equal education of girls. The ardent feminist, seeking paradoxically to deny her femininity in order to prove she was as good as a man, is now so out of date that characteristic modern girls have never even heard of her.

Once we determine to educate both men and women without partiality, there are three main ways in which it can be done. The first and the oldest way is to do it in separation. The method of separation developed naturally in America because the earliest colleges, following British experience, were men's colleges and they wished to retain their historic character. When, therefore, consciences were aroused about the educational needs of young women, it seemed reasonable to start new colleges specifically for them. The discussions attendant upon such decisions make instructive reading today, one of the best-preserved discussions being that which preceded the founding of Bryn Mawr. The original purpose was clear: it was to provide for Quaker young women something comparable to what Haverford provided for Quaker young men. Though there was no serious thought of a combined institution, the value of geographical proximity was often mentioned. In a similar way the women's colleges of New England, particularly Smith and Wellesley, were seen as almost exact counterparts of the New England men's colleges.

The second possibility is that of coeducation. This is the system adopted from the beginning in most of the state universities, being merely a continuation of that of the tax-supported schools in their areas. Coeducation is also the accepted pattern in the majority of the independent colleges, except in New England and the areas adjacent to it. In this plan of education young men and women attend all classes together, share in the same student government, occupy residence halls on the same campus, and eat in the same dining rooms. To most Americans this conception seems to be so nearly universal that it is not really a matter of argument.

A third plan is that called coordinate education. In this, the men and women have separate colleges, either in name or in fact, but they join freely in the same studies. Usually the two institutions have superior officers in common and operate under the same board of trustees, but each has its own campus, its own minor officers, its own dining facilities, its own library, and its own social organization. Familiar examples are those of Danville, Kentucky, where Kentucky College for Women is associated with Centre College, or Brown University, where the women of Pembroke have a coordinate relationship to the men of Brown. Variations on the theme are provided by Barnard at Columbia and Radcliffe at Harvard. At Duke, most of the instruction is on the men's campus, the residents of the women's campus being transported daily by bus.

All three systems now operate successfully and each presents genuine advantages. The great advantage of the separated education is that it gives the student several days each week in which attention can be concentrated upon studies, without regard to the appeal that is being made to young people of the opposite sex. For a little while both men and women can live the intellectual life, undisturbed by the rigors and pains and enjoyments of courtship. This is an important point, for the people concerned are certainly of a courting age, when interest in the opposite sex is strong and ought to be strong. That it is strong is one of the reasons for human survival. Many young women are grateful for a situation in which they have a chance to practice leadership without the competition of their aggressive brothers. They point out that when there is no separation, the young men take over the major leadership as their natural male prerogative. How often in a coeducational college is a girl the president of her class or the head of student government? There is, furthermore, the advantage gained through greater uniformity of biological age. By the end of his college career the average young man is physically mature and is the equal or superior of his sisters, but this is not true when he is a freshman. Instructors have long noted that at eighteen the girls tend to outshine the boys intellectually. When all are together, girls often seek to hide their superiority, for social reasons; but when they are taught with other girls, they can develop their intellectual interests as much as they like, without being thought queer. If they are told that it is abnormal to go through these crucial years without young men around, their answer is that all the critic needs to do is to observe what occurs on week ends. The college preacher on Sundays in a woman's college soon learns to expect a coeducational congregation.

When we turn to a consideration of full coeducation, the advantages are obvious to everyone. Since the world has both men and women in it, this may as well be faced realistically from the beginning. Women may as well learn to cope with the aggressiveness of their brothers in college, for they will certainly have to learn to cope with it later. Furthermore, the regular day-to-day working and studying together is a wholesome thing so far as potential marriage is concerned. If young people of courting age see each other only in the sentimental glow of the week end, with its football game and the big dance, they do not have an adequate chance to know each other realistically. The young man will understand his girl more honestly if he sees her, not merely when she is wearing a formal dress, but when she is struggling, perhaps helplessly, to perform an experiment in the chemistry laboratory. There is the danger, of course, of too much intimacy and too many dates of the wrong kind. Proponents of coeducation have long recognized this difficulty and face it as a calculated risk. They face it courageously because they believe the alternative risks, those of separation, are the greater. No thoughtful person rejects a system merely because it involves difficulties; before he rejects it, he weighs carefully the difficulties of any alternative of which he can think. The best system is not the one with no liabilities, for then there would be no best; the best system is that which comes out most successfully when comparative difficulties are honestly weighed.

The fact that the ordinary residential college, with both male and female students, leads normally to marriage between fellow students is neither an occasion for humor nor a defect, but a decided asset. The young person who goes to college partly in the hope of meeting and ultimately marrying a congenial mate is showing genuine maturity of judgment. Marriages are most successful when they involve a fundamental identity of background and interests. What can provide this identity better than four years of experience together on the same campus, with the same professors, the same friends, and, for the most part, acceptance of the same standards? It is not surprising to discover that marriages arising out of life in residential colleges tend to be among the most stable and enduring. The record for permanence is as striking as we should expect it to be. Once it was considered humorous to speak of colleges of the Old Siwash type as match factories, but it seems so no longer.

The advantage claimed for a coordinate system is that it combines the assets of the two other systems. It involves both separateness and togetherness. The assets are the same as those which the colleges of Oxford and Cambridge present in an extreme form. The physical nearness takes away romantic illusions, while the partial separation facilitates the growth of responsible leadership.

Whatever the comparative advantages of the three systems may be, and however profitable it is to consider them in the mood of calm inquiry, the option is no longer genuine, so far as most American families are concerned. For better or for worse, we are committed to coeducation. This is increasingly the pattern of academic life and will continue to be, so far as we can see. Harvard, so long the stronghold of separated education, now seems highly coeducational, not only because of the presence of Radcliffe students, but also because of the presence of girls in the various graduate departments and professional schools. Though universities may maintain jealously their undergraduate colleges as male preserves, women have long been welcomed or at least admitted to the other parts of university life. In like manner, men students may be admitted to graduate work in some of the women's colleges. The whole drift is in the direction of coeducation, and we could not resist it successfully even if we should wish to do so. The part of wisdom, then, is to accept this pattern, trying to see what advantages, hitherto peculiar to the other two systems, can be added to it.

There are some in our time who, because they recognize that the battle for equal education had been won, assume that no major problem remains. They make the deduction that because education for men and women should be of equal dignity and importance in a reasonable society, it should be identical. But the soundness of this deduction is by no means self-evident and may be seriously questioned. After all, the category of equality is not the same as the category of identity. Things can be equal without being the same. It does not follow from the proposition that we ought to educate our daughters as carefully and as intelligently as we educate our sons that we are required to educate them in exactly the same way. In fact, the more we contemplate the problem, the more critical we are of the concept of identity, because the lives of men and women are different in many ways.[1]

The proposition that for educational purposes we should neglect sexual differences entirely and simply treat all students, whether female or male, as human beings has a certain attractiveness until it is examined with some care. As a cliché of nineteenth-century rationalism it had a marked influence on the development both of Marxism-Leninism and militant feminism. The idea appealed to Lenin so strongly that he determined to organize the entire Communist economy on the basis of this half-truth. He recognized that this principle, if applied not only educationally but also industrially, would produce an essential doubling of the labor force. By minimizing the home, making the care of infants as well as older children and all education the responsibility of the all-engulfing state, women, he thought, could be practically as free as men to work on farms, in factories, and in offices. The inference that this

---

[1] In this connection note the conclusion in Margaret Mead, *Male and Female* (New York: William Morrow and Company, 1949), p. 383: "It may well be that the greatest intuitive gifts will be found among women."

would go far to destroy the home, making it only a dormitory, did not disturb the inheritors of the now antiquated rationalism, but seemed to them a positive advantage. The early Communists, like the early feminists, considered that they were engaged in the liberation of women. The liberation consisted primarily in the minimizing of the ways in which women and men differ, either physically or mentally or emotionally.

If the education of women is faced in an open-minded rather than a doctrinaire way, we are ready to look at the evidence to see whether the needs of men and women are identical. As we do so, we realize that there are ways in which the educational needs of men and women are the same and there are ways in which they are different. The differences appear as soon as we realize that education does not take place in a vacuum, but necessarily has reference to the kind of life people are likely to live. In many ways the life of a normal woman is far more complex than that of a normal man. So far as work is concerned, the life of most men may involve hardship, but it does not involve rapid and radical changes. Many a man finishes his formal education, enters some type of employment in which, with occasional geographical shifts, he remains until the age of retirement, and then retires. This does not occur in every male life, but it certainly occurs more often than not. The life of the average woman presents a sharp contrast to this essential simplicity. When her formal education is completed, she often takes some employment until marriage. She then marries and, even though she may continue her employment awhile, she finds that she has become involved in a whole new set of duties. Then the children begin to come and her life is as different as may be. Her new work of caring, all of every day, for little children, with their questions, their petty quarrels, their illnesses, their accidents, their early education, employs every ounce of her energy and every bit of her intelligence. However much she loves what she is doing, she is bound, if she understands her work, to have a sense of inadequacy. God never gave any young mother as much brain power as her situation requires.

The mother who understands her vocation is engaged in the task of maintaining and transmitting the intangibles without which life slips back into barbarism. She appears to be washing faces and putting children to bed, but actually these tasks are only the vehicles which are able to carry freight of varying value. The insistence of modern psychologists on the crucial character of early, or even infant, experiences only serves to stress the potential nobility of the mother's modest but dignified calling. That Saint-Exupéry understood this is shown by his description of the mother who, he says, "had taught her sons a language, handed on to them the lot so slowly garnered through the centuries, the spiritual patrimony of traditions, concepts and myths that make up the whole of the difference between Newton or Shakespeare and the cavemen." [2]

The tasks and privileges of motherhood, even though they have some preparation in the natural handicaps of pregnancy, come so suddenly that they represent a truly new chapter in a woman's life. The contrast between this chapter and that which precedes is as great as can be. Consequently, the young woman must summon a new kind of power and resiliency. To talk about really doing this work and also accepting employment outside the home is to talk obvious nonsense. Of course the central work can be neglected or it can be turned over to others, who accordingly set the basic standards of the children, but that is a different matter and requires a different discussion. Suffice it to say that, for most women, the new work is both different and consuming. It may go on for several years and then change slowly into the equally difficult but different work of guiding youthful aspirations of those who, while no longer children, are not yet adults. In all this time the woman also has many responsibilities in maintaining a home for her husband, making his hours away from his employment as happy as possible, and accepting community responsibilities, insofar as a slight margin of time permits. Then one day it dawns on the woman, now no longer young, that she has entered another period of radical change. Almost overnight, it seems, the children are gone,

[2] Antoine de Saint-Exupéry, *Wind, Sand and Stars*, p. 239.

most of the bedrooms are empty, the leaves can be taken out of the dining table, and there is *time*, wonderful time! For many women this change in the direction of more leisure is harder to bear than is the earlier change in the direction of more labor. How will this new chapter which involves both danger and opportunity be lived?

If we are agreed that this brief description of the lives of men and women is essentially accurate, it follows that the educational preparation of men and women should, in some ways, be different. Both are human beings, both feel sorrow and disappointment, and both can learn to enjoy hard work, but it does not follow that they will feel exactly the same joys or do exactly the same work. Indeed, it is obvious that they will not. The relative simplicity of a man's life requires an education suitable to its simplicity, and the relative complexity of a woman's life requires an education suitable to its complexity. Both ought to be provided and there is no clear reason why they cannot be provided in the same college. If the young man who enters college is already thinking of how his major energies are to be spent, so that, while studying the liberal arts, these arts are being organized in his mind around the practice of the law, it is equally reasonable for his sister, while studying many of the same liberal arts, to be organizing them in her mind around that noble and urgent work, the care of a family. It is as sensible for the young woman to be thinking of her vocation as for her brother to be thinking of his. And that the care of a family *will* be her major vocation is among the greatest of all human probabilities. The young men may rightly expect to get their chief vocational education *after* college, in schools of medicine, law, business, theology, or engineering, but there is no comparable expectation for the average young woman. Of course the young woman who is determined to live her life exactly as men live theirs, carrying on a profession, such as architecture or designing, in a continuity unbroken by family duties, may get her vocational training outside of college, but she is the exception. It would be foolish to act as though the exception were the rule. Most young women who attend college will be wives and mothers and most of them will not have any formal education after college days are ended.

The conception of an education which is both vocational in purpose and liberal in content has been presented and defended in the preceding chapter. This is possible for both male and female students, but it is important to say now that the education of women provides the more vivid illustration of how this is possible. A young woman who enters upon her college career with her eyes open may neither be engaged to marry nor close to an engagement, and yet may reasonably be frank enough to say that family life is what she hopes for and expects. The fact that she has not yet found her partner in this most creative of human undertakings is not itself a sufficient reason for failing to try to get ready for the life which most women experience. Perhaps, in the end, it will not come, but it is a poor kind of life which is hindered by fear of the unknown. The young medical student may, indeed, be hindered by circumstances beyond his control from practicing medicine, but the way of wisdom is to proceed boldly, recognizing how small the chance really is. The young woman, then, who leaves off her coyness and says frankly and unapologetically what she would like to be able to do is showing remarkable maturity and good sense. She is in a much stronger position than is the girl who debates whether she will have a family or a career, as though having a family were not itself a career.

The plain fact is that sometimes college education harms girls, as it sometimes harms boys. When an education harms girls, it is not because it is liberal in its intellectual emphasis, but because it is vocational in the wrong way. Girls are sometimes caused by their education to have an inaccurate picture of their own future careers. By subtle and chiefly unconscious influences they come to imagine themselves in the unbroken pursuit of extra-domestic professions, somehow unmindful of the fact that the most productive lives of most of them will be spent in a single occupation, that of wives and mothers. The colleges must be prepared today to undo the harm that they have done, a harm which is one of the disturbances of family life. It is no accident that there are many more divorces among those with college education than among those without it.

The colleges, if they will, can make a strong contribution to the recovery of family life by helping their women students to feel the true dignity of their prospective careers. The chief way in which this can be done is to help them to understand the uses of a liberal education in their peculiarly feminine pursuits. It is a sad commentary on our inadequate education to hear a recent girl graduate, asked about her present life, reply, with a hangdog expression, "Oh, I'm just a housewife." Thousands make this reply as though they were confessing failure. What many of them really mean is that they are not at the moment putting their college education to any practical use. If only the girl were practicing medicine or teaching school, the answer would not be self-depreciating at all; but when she is engaged in the most creative task of all, producing one of the particular units without which civilization is impossible, she is apologetic. This paradox is too absurd to continue among intelligent people. When it occurs with such regularity we can be sure that there is a cause, and the fault lies largely in our colleges. The fault consists not so much in what we teach or fail to teach, but in the understanding in regard to utility.

Fortunately most young women of the present generation look forward frankly and joyously to home life. Usually they are prepared to have good lives alone, if the direction of homes is not their career, though they would rather have the partnership than the aloneness. But, in addition to wanting homes, they want to feel that what they have learned in college is not wasted. It is the task of the college to make abundantly clear that what is learned need not be wasted. In a life as rich and demanding as is that of an average woman, there is use for all the literature, all the philosophy, all the scientific method, all the political science that she is ever likely to learn. But the fact that this is true does not mean that the average young woman recognizes it. The duty of the college is to provide ways in which recognition is likely to occur.

It is the duty of a college to help a girl to realize how complex her career is likely to be and how varied are the responsibilities which she will be called upon to bear. She may reasonably prepare for a short period of employment before marriage, and this is highly desirable, being helpful both to her and to society. In this period she may rightly expect to make some worth-while contribution in teaching or secretarial work or some other service which the world needs. She may also prepare for the task of managing a home with its opportunities for teaching little children in the home. She should be told how varied these duties are, including not merely cooking and cleaning and washing and sewing but also nursing and counseling and character building and playing. The mother is really the queen of a little kingdom, but she is more than queen. She is also lover and teacher and priestess. A college is derelict in its duty if it does not help young women to feel, in advance, the potential glory and dignity of this undertaking and if it does not do all it can to provide some of the resources to keep the undertaking from being the failure it so often is.

When a college has helped young women to envisage realistically yet hopefully these two chapters of their lives, it has done well, but it has not done enough. The college must also help young women to prepare for the brief periods of public service which they may enjoy in early maturity and the far more extensive periods which they may enjoy in later maturity. More and more women are able to perform important functions in practical politics, in social services, and in the formation of an intelligent public opinion. When women are set free from the care of little children, and have no economic necessity of seeking paid employment, they have a marvelous opportunity to influence the growth of civilization. All great civilizations depend, in some measure, upon the contributions of a leisure class, and mature women come nearer qualifying for this role than does any other group in contemporary society. If it were not for the work of such women, it is doubtful if we could maintain some of the really beautiful features of our culture, such as the art galleries and the symphony orchestras.

Furthermore, much of the burden of collecting funds for our mani-fold philanthropies, especially in connection with community chests, falls on women citizens. We can be thankful that there are so many women who see these needs and who have the economic freedom to work in connection with them. If all such enterprises were controlled by the state, managed by salaried officials and sup-ported by taxation, something of great value would be removed from the life we prize. The wise woman does not feel frustration and sentimental longing for the old days when she is suddenly set free from her heaviest duties, nor does she try to lose herself in the escape of continual bridge playing; instead, she looks upon her new life as a new opportunity of being creative in society. The young woman with small children may be creative in producing better people, without whom a better society is impossible, but the older woman can be creative in a wider cultural area. Both operations are needed and both should be envisaged as part of the normal ex-pectations for which college is meant to prepare.

The best preparation for these complex functions is not by con-centration upon the more utilitarian duties, such as cooking and sewing. These are not to be neglected, but they are among the duties which can be learned most easily and quickly. What is far more important is for the girl to seek training which will enable her more adequately to be a teacher in the home and a servant in the community. There is no easy and simple course which provides the requisite training in these high matters. Indeed, the studies which help most are the very studies which are known as liberal. By studying the history of art and of architecture, the girl may have a background which makes the beautification of her own home more successful. By studying literature, she will know better how to fill her home, not with cheap and ephemeral magazines or books which others choose for her, but with the books of enduring value. The presence of these everywhere, in the bedroom, in the kitchen, in the mountain cabin, is almost sure to set the standards of grow-ing children. The mother of Christopher Morley, all of whose sons became scholars, used to tell how, in their Baltimore home when the boys were small, she left books about, with apparent carelessness, particularly in those places where her sons were likely to rest after engaging in sports. The boys may not have realized that their mother was forming their taste, but she was doing so. The point is that such a task cannot be well performed unless one knows what the books are.

In a similar fashion a woman needs some good training in theology if she is to answer intelligently some of the most insistent questions which her children will ask. If God made the world, who made God? A rational answer to this childish question is available, but it is more likely to occur to the educated than to the uneducated person. How helpful if the young mother can open the Bible without confusion and undue perplexity! How good if she is acquainted with some of the classic prayers, particularly those directed to family life, like the prayers of Robert Louis Stevenson! What a blessing to have at hand materials to use in grace at table or other family devotions! But all of these are normally available in a liberal education, especially when that education is experienced in an unapologetically Christian college.

What is needed for the best education of most young women is not a set of new professional courses, but a new understanding of the relevance of existing courses. The education of girls provides the most convincing illustration of the fruitful combination of what is vocational and what is liberal, precisely because the liberal courses here serve a vocational end. All that is required is a better orientation in the minds of the college officials and consequently in the minds of the young women whom they serve. The major problem of both girls and boys in regard to liberal courses is, as we have observed earlier, the problem of relevance. They study the subjects enough to pass, but they operate at a low level of interest because they do not see the relevance to their own lives of the studies which they are forced to pursue. The best way of making relevance clear is by a vocational connection, but with the young women this connection is ready made, providing we are bright enough to see it and to explain it.

How shall this better orientation be accomplished? Only if it is taken seriously by those who both understand it and demonstrate it in their own lives. It is a great incentive in the lives of girls to be frequently in the presence of older women who have used their liberal education well in rearing families of their own, being obviously good lovers and keeping their personal attractiveness into full maturity. In looking at such persons girls can begin to have a standard of what they may become if they are fortunate and if they make the right decisions. If we were wise we should arrange opportunities in college in which the girls could meet informally and frequently with such women in order to discuss their own careers, much as young doctors meet with older doctors. The best talk is usually shop talk. It would be helpful to establish what might be called a Family House, dedicated to the dignifying of family life and providing a center for all operations to this end. Here the discussions could be held; here the counseling, providing it is of a nondisciplinary nature, could go forward; here girls could obtain practice in gracious entertainment, the serving of formal dinners, and the planning of decorations.

The building used as a center of family studies should look more like a home than a laboratory. There is as much reason for the young woman to participate in the management of a fine example of what her future center of operations will be as for a young doctor to learn in a hospital or for a young teacher to learn in a schoolroom. The Family House should be furnished with such taste that it helps to mold the taste of those intimately associated with it. At such a center there need not be many or even any new studies, but it can be a focal point which helps to give meaning to the studies already undertaken. The discussions, particularly with successful mature women, should help enormously in the right use of possible electives.

Such a plan as that just outlined is markedly different from what is now provided in most colleges. The present contributions to the subject are, for the most part, limited to two. One is the conventional program of home economics; the other is an elective course dealing with marriage and the family, a course which is sometimes given in the sociology department. The home economics department in many colleges has done good work, but in recent years it has become more and more technical, with practically no emphasis on the philosophy of home life. Paradoxically, some departments come to the place where preparation for home life is only a minor aspect of the departmental work, students being prepared, not primarily to be good wives and mothers, but institutional dieticians or teachers of home economics in high schools. In few such departments has there been any serious effort to see the opportunities of wives and mothers in their entirety.

The other solution, that of a single course in marriage, is likewise inadequate. It is inadequate because the philosophy which girls need in order to dignify their prospective lives is something which has to do with *all* their courses and not just an added one. Furthermore, in many institutions it has been fashionable to suppose that such a course, in order to be up-to-date, must be open to both men and women students. This is partly because of the notion, widely shared in the recent past, that men and women must be equal partners in the responsibility of conducting a home. This is the Leninist ideal, but that is no good reason why it should be ours. Of course fathers are parents, too, and have many responsibilities, some of which are heavy, but it is absurd to argue that there should be an equal sharing in house work or family care. There may be a few families, in unusual circumstances, in which such a division of labor is possible or even wise, but in most families it simply cannot be done. How can the young father, who works all day at the factory, have as much time to guide his children, to put them down for naps, and to wash their clothes as his wife has? He cannot do many of these tasks, not because he is above them, but because he is not present when they need to be done.

To act on the false assumption that the young father shares equally with the young mother in home management is to take away from the young mother her chief basis of dignity in her life. Of course her tasks are heavy and demanding, but that is her glory and her joy. She performs these tasks and she deserves to be honored for doing so. The wise husband will help when he can, sharing sometimes in the most humble tasks, but he will be careful to let his wife know that he recognizes her task as the greater one and that he honors it deeply. He derives satisfaction from *his* profession and she has a right to derive satisfaction from *hers*.

It is because home life is a profession for most women, as it is not for most men, that there ought to be not only times when home life is discussed *with* the young men, but also times when it is discussed *without* them. This is a feature which is part of the merit of the women's colleges and of the colleges which are coordinate, but there is no good reason why it should be denied those in coeducational colleges. The fact that it is good for men and women to be together sometimes does not mean that it is good for them to be together always. There is great merit in separate gatherings of those facing a particular calling, such as the ministry or teaching, and there is no good reason why those expecting to be wives and mothers should be different in this regard. Insofar as we love our daughters, we are eager for them to glory in being women and to take pride in the tasks, such as the teaching of little children, which in most cases they do better than men ever can. President Gettell, in his inaugural address at Mt. Holyoke, was wise in taking as his topic "A Plea for the Uncommon Woman." Certainly he helped women to be proud of being women, as men are proud of being men. At the heart of his address he said:

What we need, above all, is an intellectual experience in college that will carry through all the years and provide the foundation for a life of continuing growth and enrichment. College work should never be conceived nor presented to the student as a terminal experience nor as an escape or retreat from the larger world beyond the campus.

Nor should it be assumed for all women, as it can be for men, that college training is the preliminary step toward an uninterrupted career.[3]

President Gettell's insistence on the kind of intellectual experience which will carry through all the years is our clue. Because most educated women will engage in community service, it is highly important that they have something worth giving when they serve. Most women will perform, thousands of times, what are called menial household tasks. It is important to have such an inner spirit that these can be performed with gaiety, as a contribution to something infinitely worth while, without which the community life would wither and perish. This is best done by bringing to tasks the richest of inner resources. One young woman has said, with real profundity, that she can wash dishes more joyously with Plato than without. Men need a knowledge of great books, but a woman needs it even more. The purpose of books, as Doctor Johnson has taught us, is to help us either to enjoy life or to endure it. A woman, in the rich complexity and rapidly changing character of her life, needs all the help she can get in both enjoyment and endurance.

To a good many women there comes, through a husband's death, the sudden necessity of the radical change from a relatively sheltered existence to one in which she must be both breadwinner and mother to her children. Such an emergency cannot be prepared for specifically, because no one knows when it will come or whether it will come at all, but it can be prepared for generally. The general ability lies in the willingness to be resilient, to make adjustments without self-pity, and to use general powers in answer to a specific problem. On the whole the best assets in this predicament are not the particular qualifications for a particular job, because the particular job may not be available when the emergency arises and also because the qualifications change with the changing years. The latter is conspicuously true of teaching. The best in-

[3] Richard Glenn Gettell, "A Plea for the Uncommon Woman," *Mount Holyoke Alumnae Quarterly*, Fall 1957, p. 100.

surance for economic survival in the situation of unexpected need is a trained mind combined with the ability to express ideas clearly, a pleasing appearance, and willingness to undertake new tasks.

If education is concerned with developing resources to enable men and women to meet the challenge of the subsequent years, we must learn to think, even in the beginning, of the later years as well as the earlier ones. In our society both our male and female members can look, with reasonable assurance, to several liberated years. For men, liberation from the most strenuous employment may come at sixty-five or seventy with official retirement from business, while with most women it comes earlier, when the duties of home management are sharply reduced. We are only beginning to realize the potential richness of such years for the persons involved and the magnitude of the cultural contribution which the more mature citizens may make if they are encouraged to do so. Obviously they will not accomplish much if they sit and pine for the days of greater energy when they were obviously needed. The powers of mature people will be largely wasted unless we can develop a climate of opinion which makes people expect to do new and creative things as soon as they are set free from ordinary demands. Retirement is often resented by both men and women, but it will no longer be resented if it is seen as a chance to develop new interests which have had to wait until this glorious time for their full fruition or even their beginnings. There are many important differences between men and women, but in education for freedom there is no difference at all.

IX

The College as a Community

*"The best and most fruitful conception of a university or college
is the ancient one of a society or guild of scholars associated together
for preserving, imparting, increasing, and enjoying knowledge."*
A. LAWRENCE LOWELL

THE glory of the college consists largely in the degree in which
it deals with the entire life of those who are its members. The
fact that a college has members, and not merely attenders, tells
us a great deal about its intrinsic character. The idea of a college
is, as the name implies, the idea of a special kind of community.
It is concerned not merely with listening to lectures on history or
performing experiments in a biological laboratory but also with
hours in libraries and dining rooms and places of worship and
field houses and snack bars and dormitories. It is not merely a
place in which knowledge is conveyed.

The college exists to produce the atmosphere which will be
most conducive to the total growth of its members and this
requires the construction of a society which is intended to bring
order into the various phases of both living and learning. What
goes on in classes must, as we have insisted, be of the highest
possible quality, but the time spent there is, in any case, only a
small fraction of the total time. What we have learned is that
the cultivation of the intellectual virtues, which is our primary

131

purpose, goes on in many other ways and, for good or for ill, goes on continuously in our waking hours. There is a sense in which nothing that we do in a college is extracurricular. All of it counts, in spite of the fact that the influences, whether harmful or beneficial, may be strictly unconscious.

Though it has generally been supposed that Newman was overstating his case about the superior importance of the academic community life, there is no doubt that, by exaggeration, he made his point clear. He held that if the only choice is between an institution which has no instruction and another which, while it has instruction, has a strong social life, he would unhesitatingly choose the latter. The key passage is as follows:

I am but saying that that youthful community will constitute a whole, it will embody a specific idea, it will represent a doctrine, it will administer a code of conduct, it will furnish principles of thought and action. It will give birth to a living teaching, which in course of time will take the shape of a self-perpetuating tradition, or a *genius loci*, as it is sometimes called; which haunts the home where it has been born, and which imbues and forms, more or less, and one by one, every individual who is successively brought under its shadow. Thus . . . a characteristic tone of thought, a recognized standard of judgment is found in them, which, as developed in the individual who is submitted to it, becomes a two-fold source of strength to him, both from the distinct stamp it impresses on his mind, and from the bond of union, which it creates between him and others.[1]

The residential aspect of a college takes on immense importance, because it is a means by which the number of the practical teachers is vastly increased. The students may learn quite as much from one another as they learn from their recognized professors. The conversation, even when much of it is apparently trivial, is a means of instruction. Often students are more willing to be instructed by their equals than by their superiors, with the result that ideas on a thousand subjects are picked up in the dining room or elsewhere on the campus. This instruction is accepted

[1] John Henry Newman, *The Idea of a University* (London, 1925), p. 147.

the more willingly, precisely because it does not seem like instruction. Professor Whitehead, among the best-educated persons of our age, shortly before he died left on record a brief account of how his own college life helped him. The lectures to which he listened were confined wholly to mathematics, yet, as is well known, he matured marvelously in philosophy, in letters, and in the general understanding of the role of natural science. How was this possible? His own answer is that his interest and knowledge in such subjects arose, in the first place, out of conversations at the dining table. By slow and leisurely dining, not only with his contemporaries but also with his instructors, he was able to learn about things which, up to that time, he had not learned from books. The conversation drove him to the books and to the laboratories.

When we consider, with serious humility, the story which Whitehead tells, we have reason to be gravely disturbed about our present practice. Some good comes from our present dining habits in colleges, but the tragedy is that it is only a tiny fraction of what is possible and of what we should actually achieve if we were to take the matter seriously. One present evil is our speed. It is common to see students gulp their food as rapidly as possible, often emerging from the dining room within fifteen minutes after entering. When we ask the reason for this unseemly hurry, we get no intelligible answer. Obviously there is no time for thoughtful conversation while all are gulping.

A second evil of contemporary college dining is the widespread substitution of the cafeteria line for the served meals. Some students report that in four years of college they have never once, within the college walls, enjoyed a served meal with white cloth and decent china, linen napkins, and *peace*. How horrible to think of these young people, at the very time of life when their standards of taste are being formed, going three times every day to pick up a tray, stand in line as though at an army camp, and sit down at an uncovered noisy table in a noisy room, made even more hideous by the sound of a loud juke box. The college which settles for this is derelict in its duty, however fine its laboratories may be. Standards of taste can be lowered as well as raised and this is a way calculated to lower them, for the cafeteria is one of the easiest ways of undermining the cultivated life. It is understandable, of course, why such methods are adopted—they are cheaper. But if we comprehend what a college is and how lives are formed, this will be one of the last places where we shall economize.

Some administrators defend their failure to maintain dining service by saying that the students like it better when it is done in the quick and ugly way. Probably this is true, but it is only true in part. The students may like the cafeteria at the time, but as they look back in mature judgment, they are likely to feel that they have been cheated. Students may, indeed, resist standards of gracious living at many points, some of them preferring to sit at table in dirty sweat shirts and dungarees, but their temporary and uninstructed judgment is not the last word in the matter. Only a false understanding of democracy, which glorifies mediocrity or even vulgarity, can defend such a decision. Frequently the same student who has resisted the necessity of dressing decently for meals will be glad, afterward, that the standard has been raised. He may find that the pleasures of maturity are in some ways superior to the pleasures of adolescence.

If students finish their college careers with boorish manners, one important aspect of college life has been a failure so far as these individuals are concerned. If gracious living is not learned, why not attend evening school, which is cheaper and simpler? The best way in which gracious living is learned is by contagion, and this comes largely from those who, in their own lives, set good examples. Perhaps the saddest feature of our college dining is the fact that we tend to separate age groups. Even with trays, there could be some good table conversation between professors and students, meeting on the human rather than the classroom level, and there might be significant mutual gain. But in many institutions the instructors deliberately take their trays to separate tables or to separate rooms tacitly reserved for faculty members. The idea seems to be that they must, at all costs, avoid the kind of fellowship of which the college catalogue speaks so glowingly. Sometimes the students, instead of being grateful for the chance to pick their professors' brains in an informal way, are embarrassed by their presence and the professors are equally embarrassed. The outcome is segregation of the worst and most unproductive sort. We have a marvelous chance at academic cross-fertilization and we deliberately avoid it.

Since many colleges include a number of day students, a serious effort must be made to draw them into the total life, so that they are not cheated. There are persons who elect, usually for reasons of economy, to live in their own homes nearby. Sometimes, in consequence, they feel like poor relations, not fully accepted into college life. The part of wisdom is to encourage them to spend free time in the dormitories and to take as many meals at the college as they can afford. A conscious effort must be made, on the part of the other students, to avoid segregation on the basis of residence. A step forward would be the inauguration of one distinguished dinner a week, with good clothing, good manners, and a good program. It would not be difficult to arrange a high table and to employ a small orchestra to give tone to the occasion. Certainly the meal should be served in a mature and leisurely manner and the college schedule so arranged that there are no evening meetings on that night. Thus the temptation to run away is minimized. It would be intelligent financing to include this weekly dinner in the general charge for tuition, so that no day student stays away for financial reasons, and also to make the meal an added perquisite for all professors and for the wives of professors as well. A college which undertakes a plan of this character will show, thereby, that it understands something of its true vocation. Even if this specific plan is not adopted, the good college will do all it can to encourage faculty couples to dine in college as often as possible and thus provide, in our generation, some approximation of the good fortune which Professor Whitehead had in his.

A serious problem faced in many colleges is that presented by the existence of fraternities and sororities. These are organizations which have come to have such a large place in American academic life that they cannot be neglected. We need not consider here the function of fraternities in the large universities, where they have some justification in that they sometimes provide almost the only genuine community which the isolated and otherwise lonely student is likely to enjoy. What concerns us is the function of fraternities in colleges where the claim is that a fully integral college community already exists. Why, many now ask, introduce smaller and divisive fellowships when every effort is being made to produce a single all-inclusive fellowship? Why, in short, should we seek to spoil our own game?

The case both for and against the existence of fraternities has been made many times, but the discussion is more urgent today because of the current intense interest in trying to find the *right* pattern and not merely to defend a traditional one. Some colleges, such as those in the system of the State University of New York, have forbidden fraternities and sororities altogether and some colleges have abandoned Greek-letter societies for one sex without abandoning them for the other. Thus both Swarthmore and Stanford have disbanded sororities, but allowed fraternities to continue. The argument is that such organizations are more harmful among women than among men, chiefly because the women tend to care too much and are hurt too badly when they are not elected.

The case for the inclusion of fraternities is based on both utility and considerations of principle. The utilitarian advantage is that if the fraternities provide living quarters and dining rooms and social organization, this provision sets the college free from heavy responsibilities. At Wabash and other colleges of its type, the existence of fraternity houses saves the college a great outlay for dormitories adequate to house all of the students. The argument of principle is that human beings will form into cliques in any case and that it is better to bring some order into divisions which are bound to appear. Wisdom, then, consists in dignifying the inevitable. Many young people, it is said, are lonely at college, no matter how hard the officials try to meet their need, and this loneliness can be overcome by the effort of a small group who band together for mutual strength. Furthermore, it is held that the fraternities make a valuable contribution to gracious living, because the other residents of the fraternity house have no patience with the dirty-shirt addict. It is truly said that there is often a marked contrast between the dignity of the meals in the chapter house, with grace before meat and decent apparel, and the disorder of the college commons, where nobody feels any responsibility for maintaining a high level of manners. The fact that the officers of a fraternity are keenly aware of the opposition of those who believe fraternities no longer serve a useful purpose makes them all the more careful to maintain an appearance of respectability.

The case against fraternities involves three chief complaints, first, that those societies are divisive; second, that they harm those who are involuntarily excluded; and third, that they are un-American in their policies of racial and religious discrimination. There is a good deal of truth in each of these complaints. The charge of divisiveness is upheld by the fact that students, especially in the years after graduation, frequently show more loyalty to the fraternity than to the college itself. This is what makes the construction of palatial chapter houses possible. The answer often given is to admit that fraternities encourage the growth of small cliques, but to go on to say that human nature is made that way. There will always be better friendships among some than among others, and this occurs even in institutions which permit no secret societies. It may be necessary, therefore, to point out that the argument that a college should mirror ordinary life is not a sound argument, precisely because the college exists to challenge and improve ordinary standards.

To say that racial or religious discrimination should be countenanced on the campus because it is countenanced outside is to misunderstand seriously the entire idea of a college. The college exists not to reflect but to challenge the world. It seeks to be an island of intellectual fellowship in a sea of confusion and discrimination. The fact that there is prostitution in the outside world, and that there is some immorality within college communities, is no reason why the college should make official arrangements to encourage such practices.

The harm that fraternities and sororities do in the lives of young people who hope to be invited to join and who are not invited is serious. In some cases there are nervous breakdowns and voluntary termination of college careers, in bitter disappointment. Part of the tragedy, in such cases, is that the person may have been denied an invitation because of something extremely trivial or because of the hasty judgment of some immature person. The little snobbishness of campus social life may seem laughable to adults, but it is serious to those who are eighteen years of age and who are struggling for the support that comes from some kind of recognition.

Partly because of widespread criticism, some changes may be expected in the national policies of fraternities and sororities concerning racial discrimination, but the general practice is still that of limiting membership to those who are neither colored nor Jewish. Local chapters have been disciplined when they have sought to challenge this rule. For institutions of some types this limitation may not seem shocking or even un-American, but it is difficult to make such a practice compatible with the principles of an avowedly Christian college, since part of what it means to be a Christian is to look at each human being as a child of the same Father and to accept each, accordingly, as a person, rather than as a representative of a racial blood stream.

The decision about fraternities, like that on other controversial phases of the community life of a college, must be approached by using the method of comparing difficulties. The college without fraternities loses something; the college with fraternities loses something. On the whole, it may be said that there is little reason for introducing fraternities into a new college. Not many would welcome them if they did not already have them. This is because fraternities arose in a different age and in a situation different from our own. They arose in response to a need which does not exist in the same way in a college which takes seriously its total responsibility. The fraternities were needed in a period when the purpose of the college was not as inclusive as it is now recognized to be. They may continue to exist for a good while, because some of them are able to elicit intense loyalty, but the indications point to a declining influence in college life. The most promising experiments are those in which the fraternities are drawn deliberately into the general college pattern of residence, being allowed a partial autonomy within that pattern.

Though the residential facilities of the college have a great deal to do with the formation of student character and opinion, they are not the only aspects of academic community life that are important. One of the most important, historically, is the college chapel. Throughout most of our history the chapel bell has been the best-known symbol of the American college. That a college should provide for its members places of worship, as well as places of instruction and of residence, has been unargued during most of our heritage. For many years chapel was a normal part of each college day and attendance at it was required in the same way in which attendance was required at class sessions. That this steady impact had a great and lasting influence upon developing minds no one can doubt. One of the noble examples of it is seen in the work of the first Timothy Dwight, who often, as president of Yale, preached powerfully every day and thereby made an indelible impression upon the students. The difference between Yale College when Dwight became president and when he retired is the evidence.

In the recent past there has been a concerted and sustained attack upon the college chapel, so that it does not today have its former prominence or universality. Indeed, it is now possible to attend colleges in which the students never have the experience of chapel attendance for a single day. The decline of the chapel has come, for the most part, by making it voluntary and therefore a pure elective with no real stimulus to attendance. The result, quite naturally, is that chapel changes almost immediately from being the central, unifying experience of the campus, the one occasion which regularly brings all together, to something which seems peripheral. Young students who are given the alternative of attending public worship at which they will hear the address of some nationally prominent man, or of going to the snack bar for a soft drink and a game of cards, will, quite naturally, elect the latter. They elect it because they do not have the experience which makes rational choice possible. If one alternative is known and the other is unknown, the choice is not genuine, and this is the situation as it exists. Even though the announced speaker is a national figure as prominent, let us say, as the late John R. Mott, most of the students will have never heard of him. The fact that he was a Nobel-prize winner makes no real difference. The majority, if given the chance, would deliberately cheat themselves of the opportunity, not out of malice, but out of ignorance and immaturity of judgment. It is absurd to assume, in the beginning, the kind of judgment which the college exists to produce. Without the introduction to something better than that known in the provincial experience of the average student, the desired maturity of judgment will not be cultivated.

Whatever the outcome of the argument about the continuation

of the old American practice of college chapel, we can at least be clear that voluntary chapel is not a satisfactory solution of the problem. The alternatives are thus reduced to two: required chapel or none. The voluntary chapel normally brings only a handful of attenders and produces a situation in which everybody is embarrassed. If a college emphasizes its religious commitment in the pages of its catalogue, and, having invited a prominent religious thinker to travel six hundred miles, provides him with a congregation of thirty-one persons, part of whom are townspeople and none of whom are professors, something is seriously wrong. Perhaps it is the catalogue that should be changed! In any case the speaker will not be likely to accept the invitation to return the following year.

The easiest solution is to give up chapel altogether. After all, the college exists primarily for an intellectual purpose and perhaps it has been merely an accident of our western civilization that we have found it natural to include a religious feature at the heart of the undertaking. Harvard and Stanford and Duke and many other universities, as well as colleges, have great church structures at the focal point of the campus, but perhaps we should not arrange things this way if we were building today. Certainly they do not build this way in the Soviet Union.

If we gave up chapel altogether, we should save some valuable time for added classes, we should avoid all the headaches which arise when some students object to required attendance, and we should save the effort and money now expended in bringing to the campus recognized leaders from all over the nation and the world. The easy way is thus the way of acknowledged defeat.

Though this way would, indeed, be easy, it would be purchased at a great price, so far as the quality of the total college undertaking is concerned. It would be an overt encouragement to all who desire the complete secularization of education and would, consequently, do much to undermine the reverence which his-

torically has been so great a support to science. It would help to
split the college into departmental fragments, because the one
steady incentive to wholeness would be eliminated. It would
convince the thoughtful student that, in the eyes of the college
leaders, religion is not important. It would not seem as important,
for example, as physical training, for this, in most institutions, is
not only required but is supported magnificently. The giving up
of chapel is a public announcement that religion is a mere elective and not the dynamic center of a culture. But the most serious
liability of acquiescence in defeat would be the consequent im-
poverishment of the minds of the students. Many come from
communities in which their religious opportunities are narrowly
sectarian. In a single college, in one year, where chapel is not
only maintained but is taken seriously, students coming from a
restricted spiritual environment may be able not only to hear but
to meet personally many men of really great spiritual stature and
of national reputation. Naturally, different students will be moved
more deeply by some such persons than by others, but in the
course of four years the continuous impact of varied greatness is
enormous. Some will try to remain blasé and uninfluenced to the
bitter end, but they will need to be careful if they are to succeed
in this effort. Constantly they run the danger of becoming more
compassionate in their emotions and more universal in their intellectual interests, as well as more thoughtful about the right
conduct of their own lives.

The argument that requirement is incompatible with the nature
of religion is superficially appealing, but will not stand up under
careful analysis. The college is dealing with minds in the making
and, unless it is to retreat to the irresponsibility of the cafeteria
idea, it must establish standards which the students are not able
to establish for themselves, but for which they are usually grateful
in later years. One of the most common experiences of college
presidents is to have the very persons who, while undergraduates,
fought most bitterly against required chapel write back later

with the insistent request that it never be given up. The reason normally given by alumni is the realization, in later life, that much of the structure of their lives was formed in the chapel periods, even though they were unconscious of the fact at the time. It is sometimes said, as though this ended the matter, that people cannot be compelled to pray. This is true, but it does not follow that it is unwise to require their attendance at an occasion when other people pray. Sometimes the mood is contagious. The responsibility of the college does not extend to the right use which students make of their opportunities; the college is responsible only for the provision of opportunities and for avoiding a situation in which these will inevitably be missed. What responses are finally made are part of the fearful responsibility which no one can assume for another and which is implicit in the fact of freedom.

An added point of considerable significance is that the American academic scene is so varied that any student who is unalterably opposed to required chapel can easily avoid it. All that he needs to do is to attend an institution which accepts no responsibility in this regard. There are many of them, and our national life is such that we are free to choose. What is peculiarly irrational is for a person to choose deliberately a college which, as something intrinsic to its general philosophy, maintains required chapel and then to resist it after he arrives. If the requirement is made perfectly clear, and if its importance is stressed, the person who reads the advance announcement and then matriculates is engaging voluntarily in an implied contract. He is like Socrates, in the *Crito*, who recognizes that it would be inconsistent of him to try to circumvent the very laws to which he, by remaining, has given tacit approval. A student who fights chapel attendance after he has read the catalogue and then enrolled in a college with the historic requirement is no more worthy of our respect than the tourist who goes to Ocean Grove or Lake Mohonk and complains that he cannot use his car on Sunday.

It must never be assumed that a college which erects a chapel building and maintains a chapel service has thereby discharged its full duty in regard to the deeper life of the students. What goes on in chapel is like the hub of a wheel, which is isolated and worthless unless it is connected with the spokes. What the public worship within the college represents must reach out into the lives of both students and professors in a variety of ways. Students should be used to plan, to arrange, and to conduct public services. When given this chance they make some mistakes, as all people do, but they grow in the experience, and they grow because they are participants rather than mere spectators. Valuable as it is to bring to the campus great speakers to lift the sights of all, this practice loses much of its potential value if each occasion is a hit-and-run affair. The gain from the presence of a visitor is markedly increased if he can remain at least for a day, in order to answer questions, share in discussions, and participate in mealtime talk. Often, in these informal gatherings, a student gets an idea which changes his entire world view or intended lifework. But discussions of this type are not dependent upon the presence of visitors. Much can be done to change the atmosphere of a college by the development of small groups, some of which stress prayer, some discussion, some a special voluntary study, and some service to the community. The mood is improved by a combination of many factors, but these do not normally come of themselves. The conditions of growth into spiritual maturity, like most conditions, must be deliberately produced.

One of the finest contributions to a beneficent atmosphere is the sense of participating in a heritage. There is no doubt that age helps a college. It is good to feel a sense of membership in an ongoing tradition, because, as we share in this tradition, we become more than our puny selves. Membership, where we understand it, instills a sense of order. Because we know it *has* been done, there is reason to believe it *can* be done. To sit in a room where Thomas Kelly taught for years may not affect a good many persons, but for the sensitive it is a powerful antidote to satisfaction with mediocrity.

Nobody could have predicted, when colleges as we know them began, that organized athletics would come to occupy such a large part of academic community life. The investment in playing fields, gymnasium, swimming pool, field house, stadium, tennis courts, and general equipment is really enormous. It seems odd that a college, acknowledging its primary aim to be that of the sharpening of minds, would feel it necessary to spend so much time and energy on bodies, but such is the situation. The demands of athletic departments, beginning with the modest intention of making healthy bodies for the minds to occupy, have now achieved such dominance that coaches are sometimes paid larger salaries than are professors. The man who can put out a winning football team is, in many places, far better known and honored than are the men who are brilliant lecturers and careful scholars. What student, however great his achievement, can compare, in public estimation, with the football hero? Even to this day, there are people who do not know anything about Centre College except the fact that it beat Harvard University more than thirty years ago.

What shall we say of this surprising development? Is it a help or a hindrance in the embodiment of the college idea? The clear answer is that it is both, and both at the same time. On the positive side is the splendid way in which an athletic program can elicit the participation of students. For those on the teams, or even for those merely trying out for the teams, there is no real problem of incentive as there is in so much of our academic instruction. Furthermore, the relationship between students and coaches seems to be far better, on the average, than is the relationship between students and ordinary instructors. The coach and the team member are on the same side; the coach does not seem to the student to be one who is primarily his judge, but rather one who, at every possible point, is seeking to assist him to do better. The contact with the team representing another college is certainly one in which the older man and the younger man are partners in a single thrilling effort. Usually the coach is much admired because he is a man who, in his own undergraduate days, showed marked achievement in the very area in which he is now a teacher. Consequently, if he is a man of character, his influence on the lives of the players is both beneficent and strong. Though intercollegiate athletic competition may involve what seems like a disproportionate use of time and energy, it is a fact that something valuable goes out of the community life of a college when all of this is given up on the ground that it is nonessential. It is easy to see the evils of overemphasis on athletic competition, but it is not equally easy to see the harm that comes with its elimination. When such competition is eliminated, the college loses one of its chief cohesive forces and the male population of the student body seems to decline in manliness. This is hard to document, but not hard to observe. It is one of the reasons why some institutions have decided to reinstate intercollegiate games after having given them up for some years. The colleges which continue to support intercollegiate athletic competition, providing they do it without corruption or overemphasis, succeed in maintaining a more wholesome atmosphere and attracting a more balanced type of student. In short, the introduction of athletics into college life has not been the absurdity that it is sometimes asserted to be. Though the purpose of a college is intrinsically intellectual, the best intellectual development comes among those who are more than intellectual. Those who are likely to contribute most to national life after graduation are usually not the ones with the highest native intelligence, but those who have the ability to work and to keep going in the face of obstacles. What can be gained, in this direction, in a single hour of hard struggle on a football field is tremendous. It is good to learn that a man can go on when every part of his body cries out for rest. It is good to win and it is good to lose with grace. There are people who affect to be contemptuous of this, but they merely show thereby that something is lacking in their own lives. There is much reason to admire C. S. Lewis, particularly for his brilliant writing, but we cannot admire him equally when he says, in his autobiography, that games, in his estimation, "lead to ambition, jealousy, and embittered partisan feeling, quite as often as to anything else." [2] Undoubtedly there are ugly features of games, but the problem again is that of the alternative. Whatever the evil of games may be, the evil involved in their elimination would probably be worse.

We do not need to be advocates of the elimination of collegiate athletics to see what the temptations and dangers now are. Nearly all of the evils are those of overemphasis upon one side of life rather than any intrinsic evil. It is good for coaches to be admired, but it is absurd for them to be made as prominent as they often are. This, of course, is the fault of the sports writers, but much that is done in colleges encourages it. The whole willingness to make the big game a public spectacle moves in this direction. Without becoming bitter about athletics, the persons who care about integrity in college life must make a concerted effort to raise the prestige of other forms of excellence. Winning a debate must be made as important as catching a forward pass, and part of the means of doing this is a better balance in publicity.

At the present time great harm is done young athletes by encouraging them to think of themselves as much more important than they are. An eighteen-year-old boy who may be ignorant and intellectually lazy often supposes that he is a truly valuable addition to some college, merely because he was on a successful basketball team in some high school. Having an unrealistic opinion of his own worth, he becomes insufferable and may be spoiled for life. He supposes that colleges are competing for the priv-

[2] C. S. Lewis, *Surprised by Joy*, p. 129.

ilege of enrolling him as a student; and when he visits an office
of admissions, asks, not what it will cost him to attend, but what
the college offers.

Ridiculous as is the posture of the ignorant boy waiting for
offers, we cannot blame him wholly, for the action of some
colleges has encouraged his false estimation of his own importance.
Some colleges, because they are overeager for the esteem which is
associated with winning teams, actually go out into the open
market to find the prospects. In one American college, unbeliev-
able as it may sound, the basketball coach is given an annual
fund of $32,000, which he can use to employ players and for
which he is not required to make any accounting at all. That
such a practice makes the American college a laughingstock,
particularly in foreign eyes, goes without saying. The worst of it
is that the very college which has the big fund for basketball
players pays low salaries to its professors. The time has come
to label such practices as corruption and to eliminate them at
whatever cost. It would be better to lose every game than to
lose integrity.

Overemphasis upon athletic competition encourages not only
false standards of prestige and financial inequity but also a real
diminution of intellectual achievement. Obviously, a boy who
is traveling two thousand miles to play a game is not going to
do a full week's work in his studies. One would have to be naïve
to believe that the mere act of carrying some books along means
that real intellectual work is done. Anyone who thinks that serious work is done by the members of the Big Ten team which
annually spends all of December in southern California preparing
for the Rose Bowl game is really weak in his understanding of
human nature. The upshot is that, for many of the students
who are involved in an overemphasis on athletic competition,
intellectual life suffers and suffers severely. In supposedly good colleges the basketball games, in a single winter, number as many as
twenty-one, about half of these necessitating trips of some dura-

tion. If the players get good grades under these circumstances, the persons who give the grades are, in most cases, simply failing to maintain high standards of excellence. The harm of too many games is also felt by the student body in general, which often is moved by loyalty to attend even on a week night, with the consequence that the paper due the next day is a poor, trivial production, more like the work of a child than an adult.

The way out of this predicament lies not in the elimination of athletics, but in the courage to maintain competition and yet keep it within reasonable limits. Those who guide policy must have the courage to refuse to buy players, even though the refusal insures a few more defeats. They must likewise have the courage to limit the number of contests, even if this means elimination from a conference in which the other teams demand an excessive number of encounters. Equality of competition can be secured by limiting contests to those colleges in which there is an equal determination to resist, at all costs, the current academic corruption. It ought not to be difficult for those with the same standards to find each other and thus to restore genuine competition rather than mere slaughter. It is possible to have excellent play on the part of students all of whom pay their own tuition and do not feel like employees. Furthermore, by eliminating the hired players, we give some chance of participation to the ordinary decent students who constitute our main field of responsibility. It is certainly better to give the joys of intercollegiate play to a well-rounded boy who is nevertheless far from being a professional athlete than to give all the chances to the paid player who may be far from well-rounded in his interests. It is better to bring out the powers of the person who is already a loyal member of the total community than to give preference to one who has no interest in the community. There is no reason why participation in athletics should be a handicap to a student who needs scholarship aid. Scholarships should be given, not as advance rewards for prospective play, but solely on the basis of general worth or general achievement. The only way to avoid corruption is to separate the scholarship aid completely from the administration of athletics, though it is right and fair that those on the scholarship award committees should be as friendly to the athletic program as they are to the other legitimate features of college life.

One of the worst mistakes of college football is the practice of housing the team members in a separate building, with separate meals, as though they were a group of racing dogs in need of special care. The result of this expedient is to fragment, even more, what ought to be a community spirit but is not. The glory of athletics is that athletic competition, rightly guided, may contribute beneficially to the atmosphere by which men and women are best developed. If competition fails to do this, or if it destroys rather than encourages the reality of community, radical changes must be made.

Because we do not understand the meaning of a college apart from community, we need to know what community is. A community is not merely a number of people, such as those sitting in an air terminal. The people at Idlewild, for example, are far from constituting a community. A group is not a community until it is marked by a basic identity of ideals and standards. It is a group of people who, though they may not know all of the same things, *care* about the same things. It is not merely a matter of common activities, though we often act as though it were. Some activities there must be, but we have too many of them, so many, indeed, that the lives of many prominent students are hectic. They do not have time to study because they are always doing something or going somewhere.

Most colleges have too many clubs and far too crowded schedules. We compete with ourselves! The consequence is that if an excellent orchestra is brought to the campus, the attendance may be embarrassingly poor. This is not primarily because most of those who stay away do not care for good music, but chiefly because they have to be, that night, at the Chess Club or the

Riding Club or the Photo Club. We shall not have real community on a campus until we bring order into our total life, cutting down, not only on the number of hours spent in classes, but also on the number of hours spent in the pursuance of ends which, though not evil, are unduly confusing and competitive.

Curious as it may seem, some of the best educational progress is made in summer sessions, because the outside activities are then largely in abeyance. A student reports, with surprised joy, how delightful it is, in a summer session, to be able to read, to study, and to think, without dashing off to attend the meeting of the sorority or to share in the basketball pep rally. The paradox is that we have encouraged the development of a host of activities in order that they may help to build up the reality of community life, with consequent moral and spiritual growth, but frequently we succeed only in killing the thing which we love. Community we must have, if life is to be good, but the community is ruined when the group activities become too numerous or when any of them get out of line because of excessive emphasis. Hope lies in the continual vigilance which maintains a sense of order.

X

The College in the Community

"Liberty cannot be preserved without a general knowledge among the people."

JOHN ADAMS

Every contemporary college is in some community. A few colleges are located in great industrial cities, but most of them are not so situated. Some are in beautiful academic villages like the famous ones of Ohio, Oberlin, Granville, Oxford, and Gambier. Many more are in medium-sized cities, surrounded by several thousand citizens, with some industry. All, by virtue of modern automotive transportation, are easily accessible to nearby urban centers, even if they are in the country. Davidson now belongs to Charlotte, Guilford belongs to Greensboro, and Simpson belongs to Des Moines, even though all once seemed to be totally separated from these cities. Wabash belongs to Indianapolis as truly as it belongs to Crawfordsville. This change in accessibility, which arises from new modes of transportation, is almost as great as a change in location and it requires, on the part of each college, a new examination of its contemporary role.

There is a sense in which each of the colleges just mentioned is national in its responsibility, since students and professors come from a wide area, but this is not incompatible with the other sense

152

in which each is part of the local scene. The college, like the individual, can profit from a careful consideration of the theme "My Station and Its Duties." [1] It is only when a college has some understanding of what it *is* that it can begin to know where its responsibility lies. It must serve the nation by helping to maintain a high level of national taste and by producing persons of such merit that they contribute to the national scene, but it must, at the same time, become a center of beneficent infection where it is. The college is failing if there is not a noticeable cultural improvement in the life which surrounds the campus.

In this connection it is profitable to consider the contrast between a college and a prison, in the effect of each upon a community. The prison is usually a large and formidable structure, costly and handled with efficiency, but in no sense does it belong to the community. Apart from the fact that the prison employees live in the nearby town and therefore spend their wages and salaries in it, the prison does not affect the major life of the community at all. It has a wall around it, both physically and spiritually. Whereas the prison is a cultural enclave, the college, by contrast, has no wall. The students and professors mingle with the community, attending its churches, joining its clubs, and sometimes taking part in its local government. Consequently the influence of a good college is felt in many ways, including the appreciation of art and music and respect for excellence in all educational endeavors. [2]

The ways in which a college may use its facilities to permit the surrounding population to participate in the total college life are many and varied. Those whose time will permit may attend college convocation and hear, thereby, speakers of outstanding reputation not normally available in an ordinary town. Without any harm to the residential students, townspeople may borrow the books of the college library, visit museums, attend musical concerts, share in

[1] The title of a famous philosophical essay by F. H. Bradley of Oxford.
[2] Fifty years after the closing of most of the old academies, particularly those of the Middle West, it is possible to notice a real difference between those communities which once had academies and those which had none.

art exhibitions, and engage in religious worship in the college chapel. Scholars may be employed for special tasks in local industries, local teachers of the public schools may confer with academic leaders in their fields, and interesting athletic opportunities may be provided in the field house or the gymnasium. Thus the college is practically certain to influence the community mightily. The economic influence, alone, is greater than we usually realize. A small college with 750 students, each spending $2,000 each college year, brings, in this way alone, a million and a half dollars of outside money into a community. This, however, is not to be compared with the contribution of ideas.

If our conception of the college as an institution engaged in the task of maintaining and elevating the level of civilization is correct, we have, thereby, a fairly clear understanding of what the right relationship between the college and the external community is. Each college has a primary obligation to the life nearby. The scholar's greatest responsibility is not to mankind in general, which in any case becomes an abstract entity, but rather to those nearest to him, particularly his own children. He is most deeply responsible to those who have a valid claim upon him. If each man were to discharge his responsibility to those nearest to him, we should begin to have a decent world. Likewise, in view of the fact that our colleges are admirably spaced in our total American population, we should be able to advance mightily if each college were to be a truly civilizing influence in the immediate area which it serves. Responsibility does not end at home, but it begins there. The entire area can be lighted, if the lights are rightly spaced and if each is truly burning.

The conception of a college as a center of light in its community is an old one, signified in many institutions by the words on the college seal, but now a new factor is added in the immense importance of adult education. Since we have only begun to see what this may mean, we can be sure that far greater changes are in store in the immediate future. The concept of higher education for those of older years may be as revolutionary in educational theory as is a new invention in technology. The conventional pattern for many years included the unexamined idea that education is primarily suitable for the young; now we realize that this may not be valid at all. Indeed, we realize, with something akin to a revelation, that education is far too good a thing to be limited to the young. Why should it not go on, with increasing power and joy as long as the individual lives? If learning is a basic and not a temporary human satisfaction, there is no reason to set arbitrary bounds to its development.

A number of factors have combined to make a radical reassessment of the matter of age in educational pursuits. One factor is the realization that older people can learn and can learn with great speed. A man of forty whose intellectual interests have been maintained can learn a new language faster than he could have at twenty. There are several reasons for this, including the likelihood of a stronger motive at forty than at twenty. Thus contemporary journalists have reported the speed with which, as adults, they have learned to read and speak Arabic. A man who has long engaged in the habit of learning is a better learner. Though many of our adages are false, few are as obviously false as the saying that it is impossible for an old dog to learn new tricks. As applied to humans the adage simply is not true.

Another factor in our re-examination of the right age for education is the recognition that some things, of great value, cannot be appreciated apart from experience. It may be right to introduce young people to the classics, but there is no doubt that much of the meaning, particularly of the deep pathos, is wasted upon them. Every thoughtful adult can assent to Louis Kronenberger's dictum, in his introduction to the *Portable Johnson and Boswell*, that "one must be a good way past youth to appreciate the great virtues of Johnson himself." The prayers of the great lexicographer are among the most profound in any language, but it is idle to expect most young people to appreciate them, because most of the young people have not experienced enough defeat to know what Johnson is saying in the magnificent manuscripts which lie in his old college. The grown man may be deeply moved and, indeed, his life changed, as he prays, with Johnson, "that, when I shall render up, at the last day an account of the talent committed to me, I may receive pardon," but we have yet to discover a youth of twenty who responds similarly to such words.

It is not easy for most men and women in middle life to engage in higher education as a full-time pursuit, no matter how keen their intellectual desires may be. This is because they have the responsibility of caring for their children and doing the creative work of the world outside the college halls. Sometimes they are sad when they think of the academic opportunities which they once had. They are ashamed as they realize how, earlier, with no serious interferences, great opportunities were wasted. It is conceivable that in a truly rational society we might well reverse the roles, letting those from eighteen to twenty-two work in the factories and, ten years later, be given a similar period of freedom from employment, in order to carry on studies at a time when they could be more adequately appreciated and assimilated. Pending such a radical change, which is not likely to be adopted, we have another alternative in the use of such freedom as modern society makes possible, even for those who are fully employed.

The new leisure which comes as a result of automation, and the revived interest in adult education, are two factors which combine perfectly. With the short work week for those employed, and with the use of automatic devices in the home to relieve the housewife of some grueling labor, modern men and women have a prospect of leisure such as the human race has never experienced in its long past. Everyone knows that the gift of leisure does not guarantee a good use of it. People can waste it by sitting endlessly and passively, watching television programs, or they can go to the bar or they can attend the drive-in theater night after night, watching one juvenile picture after another. But it is also possible to use leisure to develop some new skill, some new interest, or some new learning. And this planned development need not be limited to four years, as we have normally supposed in the recent past; it can go on for all of a lifetime.

Most men and women see their world through only a tiny crack. It is by education, and the reading and thinking which education encourages, that this crack can be widened. What *has* been done, can be done. If others of modest endowments have learned some of the secrets of atomic physics, so can I, providing I am really interested in doing so. At the outset the study looks formidable, but it ceases to seem so formidable if we are willing to take one step at a time. All that we really need to do is heed the famous Cartesian wisdom of taking the simple steps before we try to take the complex steps, and also of dividing a complex problem into manageable units.[3] What others have learned in any field of inquiry can be learned again. People differ in brilliance, but they do not differ, normally, in the essential ways in which their minds work.

The result of this combination of factors is that, today, the evening classes of many colleges are quite as well attended as are the day classes, and the dignity of the work given in them grows every year. Since we have touched only the fringe of this movement, it is reasonable to expect that the time will come when the evening colleges normally surpass day colleges in numbers of students.[4] The new pattern which is emerging is that of continuous education in which a person may be both a student and worker, with no necessity of choosing between the two phases of life. Modern transportation makes it wholly feasible to draw evening students, of both sexes, of many occupations, and of various ages, from an area with a radius of fifty miles and this, in coming years, may be extended. Furthermore, as the college feels more and more responsibility for guiding

[3] René Descartes, *Discourse on Method*, Part II. The rules alluded to are the third and second of Descartes.

[4] George Williams College of Montreal, a college established by the Young Men's Christian Association, reports an enrollment of 9,400.

the intellectual life of its area, branch evening centers can be set up at various key points. The instructors can go to Centerville on one night and to Lewisburg another, repeating the instruction in a different center. Some professors who have the vision of what can be accomplished in this way will not resent giving a few evenings each week, particularly if they can be given freedom, during the daytime, to pursue their own study and the writing of books.

One promising development in colleges is the inauguration of instruction in the art of management, offered for students who are fully employed. The class must meet in the evening and may continue for a full college year. The instruction given is not merely utilitarian, in the narrow sense, because the growth which industrial managers need, and which some of them realize that they need, is to be found on another level. The men seem to be helped by studies which have no apparent connection with the factories in which they are employed, but which tend to deepen their lives and to widen their interests. It is something of a revelation to see how a class in management can take hold of the *Pensées* of Blaise Pascal.

If this new conception is to succeed, a high level of expectancy and of requirement must be maintained rigorously. Adult education misses the mark if the classes are nothing but entertaining lectures in which the professors amuse the citizens and require no work on their part. Neither in youth nor adulthood can education reveal its true value unless the student works industriously and creatively. Learning cannot be given; it must always be earned. It does not come by passive listening. If our adults attend evening classes in the same passive mood in which they listen to addresses at the women's club or the luncheon club, the great new conception of continuous education is frustrated. Since real education is self-education, all that the instructor can do is to arouse people to undertake this lonely task. The social aspect is necessary, but it is not sufficient; it provides a certain amount of yeast, but the individual student still has to bake the bread.

There is a serious temptation on the part of the instructor in adult college work to lower the standard because the members of the class may have been out of intellectual activity for a while and may also be tired, as a result of other duties during the day. Experience shows, however, that older people can maintain the standard normally expected of full-time students if time is given for them to get into the swing again, and if much is expected. It is especially important for such older students, if they are to grow, to try to take excellent notes, following a scholarly method, and not sit like members of the audience while the professor does all the work. If all that we have is pleasant evening lectures on poetry or art or scientific method, the potential cultural revolution will fail to take place. It is as true in the evening as in the day college that science cannot be learned without serious laboratory work.

The community classes, then, must be scholarly undertakings. The students must write and produce and participate. Many, as a result of this serious task, can prepare themselves to be the teachers of others, thus solving one of the chief problems of adult education, the shortage of adequately prepared teachers. This is important because we can predict that as the new idea takes hold all over the nation, the continuation of education becoming the accepted way, the shortage of teachers may easily become more acute than it now is. The only solution lies in making the experiment of adult education humanly self-sustaining. Those who have been helped to enter a new and more interesting life by this means have a responsibility to help others. By altering one term in Dr. Schweitzer's famous conception, we may have in effect, the "fellowship of those who bear the mark of *ignorance*." [5] All those who have borne this mark, and have in some degree been liberated from it, are duty bound to set free as many others as possible.

[5] See Albert Schweitzer, *On The Edge of the Primeval Forest* (London: A. & C. Black, Ltd., 1924), pp. 173–176. "The man" says Schweitzer, "who, with a doctor's help, has been pulled through a severe illness, must aid in providing a helper such as he himself had, for those who otherwise could not have one." The idea that we pay our debt of gratitude only by helping someone else seems to the African doctor to be really profound as well as practical. The good man never lets the chain reaction stop with him.

Another way in which the college can serve the community is in educational assistance to those in old age, including those retired from active employment. As we have seen in an earlier chapter, retired people now constitute one of the chief unexploited resources of our current civilization. Of the babies being born now, it is predicted by reliable medical scholars that, because of the remarkable improvements in public health, many will live to be a hundred years old or more. Barring a major catastrophe, this outlook now seems beyond serious doubt. What about the thirty years or more which are thus available? Shall they be wantonly wasted or unused? We are not that rich. We must use all of the disciplined imagination we can muster to make sure that these added years are years of growth and of service to the community. One obvious plan is that of the learning of new skills. Thus a first-class electrical scholar, one of the inventors of the mercury-vapor lamp, now in retirement, has learned what for him is something wholly new, the cutting and polishing of beautiful stones. He has assembled the equipment, studied the books, developed a stone collection, and now has an exciting new chapter in his life. Why not? All that others need, for similar new chapters, is the idea, the incentive, and the availability of the requisite information. The electrical scholar has had all this partly because he lives in close proximity to an excellent institution of higher learning.

Many people go through the middle periods of their lives burdened with many duties, but never wholly forgetting some secret ambition. The free years of older life, liberated from the necessity of earning by the existence of social security and pensions, provide the perfect opportunity for the satisfaction of secret creative desires. The college can be of marvelous service in assisting individuals in the satisfaction of these desires.[6] Perhaps a man has had to give his time to selling insurance, but has had all along a desire to play a violin. His years of freedom may, with the help of a college, be the

[6] Boston University now offers free tuition to men and women over sixty-five years of age.

years in which he finds joy in trying to do what he always wanted to do, but could not. Though people in middle life are practically bound to limit their continued education to evening hours, this is not necessary among retired people. There is no reason why some of advanced years should not enroll as regular full-time students. Perhaps we shall eventually build college dormitories for older people where they have the society of their contemporaries and a mutual interest in learning. Some may consider the idea fantastic, but perhaps that is only because it is comparatively novel. The serious question is whether there is anything intrinsically wrong with the conception. As education becomes increasingly important in our competitive civilization, we may be called upon to think of many things of which we have never thought before. The educational frontier is still expanding.

Though many parts of our civilization can help to produce higher expectancy regarding older years, the responsibility of the college is greater than that of most institutions. The college should stir up so many desires in people that an entire lifetime will not suffice to give opportunity for their full satisfaction. The instructors should talk so temptingly of a host of books that it will take all the years there are to read them. If you now pick up, for the first time, a book of which you heard good things forty years ago, this is a perfectly reasonable operation. There was no time for it earlier, but now perhaps there is. What a joy it would be not to be employed at all, because this would entail the possibility of self-employment. Then you could start, in earnest, to learn Japanese, to read all of the writings of Edmund Burke, to visit African ports in a freighter, to start painting. No person who has encountered any real education can ever find time hanging heavy on his hands.

The older years are especially appropriate for reading the older and better books. No sensible man shows anxiety about reading new books. He knows that they will wait and that nearly all of them will be forgotten in five years. If a new book happens to be easily available he may read it, but in doing so he is likely to resent the time it steals from the well-tried works which will not be forgotten in five years or in fifty. It is one of the glories of literature, in contrast to merchandise, that the term "secondhand" is, in literary usage, a term of respect.

Another community group which has not usually been looked upon as part of the college responsibility, but which the college may serve, is that made up of children. Childhood has never been easy to live through, and presumably never will be, but the lot of the modern child is in some ways far more difficult than was the corresponding lot a generation ago. The central problem of the modern child is that he has nothing to do and little to challenge him. The young person sitting on the stool at the drugstore soda fountain and saying dolefully that he has absolutely nothing to occupy his time is really a sad and frightening sight. There were reasons for passing laws restricting child labor, but the result is by no means uniformly good. A large part of juvenile delinquincy arises directly from the fact that the parents work to keep children in idleness, when work is what the children need to dignify their young lives. So long as our major pattern of life was agricultural, this was no problem. The farm boy of an earlier generation sometimes felt sorry for himself because he wished for time to swim or to loaf, but there were always more weeds to pull, more hay to harvest, more animals to feed, more cherries to pick. Not only were his summers thus dignified by the fact that he was seriously needed if the family farm was to prosper and the bills were to be paid; he was also needed during the school months because of the endlessly recurring chores. There was never any doubt in his mind about the necessity; if milk is to be produced the cows have to be milked, and they require milking on the night of the game just the same as at any other time. Such a life was demanding, but it was never soft. The picture of endless entertainment of the young on the part of their elders was not even imagined.

All of us know that however damaging the idleness of modern youth may be, we cannot reverse the process. Earlier generations of children had the problem of too much labor and contemporary children have the problem of too much freedom from toil, but the old days will not come again. We are not likely to put our children into factory labor and even the old family farm is, as a result of mechanization, practically a thing of the past. Most farm boys today have never used a pitchfork or built a stack of wheat. The elimination of the grain binder has been as revolutionary a change as was its introduction.

Since we shall not go back, and since the present situation is intolerable, we must try to produce a better future. In the words of Lincoln, "If we could first know where we are and whither we are tending we could better judge what to do and how to do it." For one thing, we can reverse the process which makes the education of children both empty and easy, by demanding longer hours and more months in school and also by requiring genuine study in after-school hours. The parents could help by demanding that the children do the scholastic work that is required instead of doing it for them or, worse still, complaining about it. But even then there is still a great deal of empty freedom. This is where the college of the community has an opportunity. In nearly all communities the college has the only first-rate scientific equipment for miles around. To the normal child this is fascinating. The healthy-minded child is naturally interested in a telescope, for example, and usually a college has a good one, which is used only a small portion of the available time.

The college, if it is alert to the problem of the unemployed child, can bring some vital interest into his life by organizing science clubs, with regular opportunities to make use of the laboratory and observatory equipment.[7] Such a procedure catches the young person's imagination at a period of his life when he is not yet ashamed to seem eager. There is no telling how deeply such experiences may influence future decisions, including vocational ones. The

[7] See the editorial on this conception in the *Saturday Evening Post* for August 3, 1957.

plan, therefore, does more than to keep children out of mischief. It is more than a harmless alternative to vandalism and gang fighting. It is something which, if seriously undertaken, might do much to overcome the present shortage of persons devoted to scientific pursuits. If conducted by the right people, it would help to alter the prevailing unflattering picture, in the minds of youth, of what a scientist is. Too many now think of the scientist as a true intellectual descendant of Thales, gazing at the stars and consequently falling into an open well. Moreover, the early experience of familiarity with a college campus might encourage some children who would otherwise have avoided it to carry on their higher education as far as possible. It might help some to arrive later at college, better prepared than they would otherwise have been, and to profit by what a college has to give because more willing to learn. At the same time this undertaking makes excellent use of college students, whose own training is improved as they try to teach the children who enroll in the project.

Both the college and the surrounding community can profit by a conscious attempt at mutual aid. The college is a better college if it does not have a spiritual wall around it, and the community is a better community if it accepts the college as part of itself. Already we see a number of ways in which the mutual assistance can be beneficent, but we can be sure that there are other ways of which we are not yet aware. Here, then, is a cultural frontier in which new developments may be expected with confidence and with hope.

XI

The Achievement of Academic Integrity

"That academical honours, or any others, should be conferred with exact proportion to merit, is more than human judgement or human integrity have given reason to expect."
SAMUEL JOHNSON

THE educational philosophy which stresses the idea of community is sound, but it is dangerous if it is expressed in such a way that it seems to minimize the supreme importance of intellectual discipline and achievement. Though a college is not merely a place for the imparting of knowledge, it is failing in its function if knowledge is not imparted. Therefore it is important to make clear that no good college can fulfill its function by being a place of mere fellowship without toughness of intellectual fiber. Part of the educational purpose is to know, and this purpose is not likely to be achieved unless there is some reasonably accurate means of learning *whether* people know. A college, if it is to justify the tremendous expenditure of time and energy and money and sacrifice which it represents, must be dissatisfied with the creation of a country-club atmosphere. There must be times of reckoning, as well as times of opportunity, if we are to have academic integrity.

Though men make mistakes in judgment, judgment has to be rendered. There is one thing worse than erroneous judgment and

165

that is absence of judgment. If no distinction is made between shoddy work and careful work, the entire academic enterprise falls apart. Of course it would be nice if everyone would work for the love of the work and put out energy willingly, even though there were no fear of failure in the course or of elimination from college, but human nature is not made that way. Since human beings are constitutionally lazy, they require a multitude of stimuli to work at any level comparable to their capacity. A college operating on a basis of nothing but generosity, giving degrees to all regardless of the quality of achievement or lack of achievement, would soon be a college granting worthless degrees. The fact that a graduate has a piece of paper does not of itself mean much; a degree can be almost as lacking in value as is Confederate money. However much we may hate examinations or point out their flaws, an educational institution without any examinations or with easy examinations would soon lose its academic reputation, though its playing fields might be beautiful and the atmosphere of its chapel devout. Tenderness without a mixture of toughness is fundamentally unkind.

Sometimes we deplore competition, especially when we see students fighting for the top places in a class or for the highest scholastic honors. Some critics have even supposed that the announcement of honors is somehow undemocratic because it makes those who do not receive honorable mention feel inferior. The deep error in such a philosophy of democracy is that it leads inevitably to mediocrity. A society in which mediocre work brings as much recognition as does excellent work will become a mediocre society, sooner or later. This will occur because human life is intrinsically imperfect and therefore needs all of the stimulus it can get. We ought to be thankful for academic competition and sad because there is so little of it. Victory is undoubtedly a good, but victory is impossible without competition. Tennis is a marvelous game, but it would soon die out if it consisted merely of bouncing balls against a wall and hitting them again. Much of the joy of the game is involved in the fact that the opponent also hits the ball, and the excitement comes in the effort to hit it better than he does. Heaven will be a bit disappointing if all such competition is denied its residents.

Competition of a sort not widely different from that possible in academic settings is now becoming a factor of extreme importance in world affairs. The two great Communist countries, Russia and China, have undertaken international cultural and industrial competition in dead seriousness. Communist China, encouraged by her leaders, has named Great Britain as her competitor, particularly in industrial development. Soviet Russia has chosen the United States as her opponent, the people being daily urged to surpass the people of the United States in pure science, in technology, in music, in athletics, and in standard of living. Only in the light of this acceptance of competition can we understand the concentration of effort which enabled Russian technicians to put into orbit not only the first artificial earth satellite but also the first artificial solar planet. The accomplishment had its scientific aspects, but science did not provide the major incentive. The overriding purpose was not the verification of a scientific hypothesis, but a sense of international victory. The effort was not merely to launch satellites, but to beat America. A motive as powerful as this must not be discarded, but wisely used.

Examinations are intrinsic to the learning process for at least four reasons. The first reason is that the prospect of an examination gives a powerful incentive to learning. The student often seems to accomplish more in one week immediately prior to an examination than he accomplishes in ten weeks before that. In getting ready to answer definite questions, he realizes how vague his knowledge has been and he sees to it that it becomes more precise. He looks over a field and sees where the major gaps in his knowledge are. He consquently fills these gaps as best he can. Preparation for an examination is sometimes the most successful part of a year's learning because the incentive which the prospect of testing provides leads to self-directed education. The student who wants to succeed does not need an instructor to tell him what his weak points are; he recognizes them easily and, if he means business, sets to work to strengthen these points. Frequently the result is that the entire course begins to come alive in a few days. Suggestions made in lectures or in discussions which meant almost nothing at the time when they were originally given suddenly take on significance in the light of the whole process. Facts which were learned lightly the first time may now, as a result of intensive review, be learned so deeply that they will remain in consciousness for life. The second learning may have a disproportionate result.

A second valid reason for holding examinations is that they give some reasonable basis of judgment concerning what the student has accomplished. Accomplishment may be recognized in many ways, but the other ways are inadequate apart from direct questioning. The professor who judges only on the basis of participation in class discussion may easily be deceived by a facile tongue. A boy may sound wiser than he is if he can pick his topic and if he can make quickness of mind a substitute for careful preparation. The examination, whether oral or written, though admittedly imperfect, is the best known way of determining whether or not a student is bluffing. It gives a chance to the careful person who does not have the self-confidence to be a brilliant conversationalist, but who nevertheless knows what he is talking about and can explain it if he is given a fair chance to do so under circumstances suitable to his own personality.

A third reason for examinations is the consequent satisfaction which they may bring to the student, particularly in later years. Some critics of examinations, even though they never suggest any genuine alternative, are emotionally opposed to tests of all kinds, but, apart from such persons, the remembrance of an examination well met is a source of deep satisfaction. The student who has prepared diligently is glad to be tested, and if because of various factors he has been able to resist the temptation to cheat, he can take pride in his achievement as long as he lives. It is surprising, in view of the supposed opposition to examinations, to find that sev-

eral good students look back on their periods of testing as the happiest occasions in their academic careers.

A fourth reason for holding examinations is that an instructor,
after studying the answers given, can be guided by them to do
better teaching in the future. He can see, as a result of the examination, where the student is weak and where the instruction
failed to make some points really clear. Since the professor knows
that in one sense it is he who is being judged, having had his
opportunity with the students, he accepts the results with a certain
humility. He sees the student as an individual for whom he is par-
tially responsible and he decides, in the light of examination
results, what his next step in guidance should be. Often the examination reveals some glaring weakness which he did not at all suspect, and would never have known apart from this mutually
humbling experience. He may be surprised to learn, as a result
of the failure to answer a question, that the student has never read
a word of the writings on which the entire course has been based.
In making such a revelation possible, the system of examinations,
whatever its minor difficulties, is amply justified.

Once we accept the conclusion that a college is a society which
must examine as well as teach, we are driven to consider carefully
the comparative value of the different forms which examinations
can take. One result of the recognition of human inadequacy, including the fallibility of the subjective judgment, has been the
emergence of a system known as "objective tests." The purpose of
these is to eliminate the personal factor, so far as the professor or
the examiner is concerned, and thus provide something which is
equally fair to all. The device by which this laudable purpose is
supposedly accomplished is that of giving several possible answers,
one of which is claimed to be the correct answer and the others
incorrect. All that the person being examined, then, has to do is
to check one answer and the result can be computed by mechanical means. This seems to be easy on all concerned. The student
is not required to write one word of any language and the person

who sets the examination is mercifully set free from reading one hundred long answers to the same question. Because of these obvious advantages the method is now widely used, so much used, in fact, that some students report that they have never been examined in any other way than this.

In spite of the advantages mentioned, it is necessary to point out that the general use of nothing but multiple-choice answers leads to intellectual decline rather than advance. The essential fault is that the method trivializes whatever it touches. It may test a certain superficial kind of knowledge, but this is not the knowledge which a college is organized to impart. Questions which can be answered by a mere yes or no are inevitably oversimplified. "Was Luther loyal to the medieval Christian heritage?" Anyone who is led to suppose that such a question can be answered simply has been given a distorted historical picture. Luther was extremely loyal to some of the aspects of the medieval heritage and was extremely critical of others. What is important to know is *which* he accepted and which he rejected, and why. No answer to such a question which can be computed on a machine is really worth making. It may seem desirable, in a gadget age, to reduce everything to computation devices without the flexibility of expression which mature language makes possible, but it is hard to think why the leaders of a college would make this fundamental error of judgment.

The deep fallacy in what are known as objective tests consists in the acceptance of the false assumption that the subjective judgment can be eliminated from the human situation. Undoubtedly the computing machine is free from subjectivity, but how about the person who sets up the alternatives to be checked? Does he have some mechanical or infallible means of determining in advance the relative worth of a yes here and a no there? If not, subjectivity has not been avoided, and the system is misnamed. Who is to say whether the comparative possibilities are of equal worth? Gilbert Highet has shown how questionable the basic assumptions of objective testing are by using the illustration of questions about

Simon Peter. The four possibilities about Peter's identity might be:

(1) soldier
(2) rich Pharisee
(3) poor fisherman
(4) well-to-do farmer

"These answers," says Highet, "are set out as though they were equal. Whoever answers (3) is right. Whoever answers (1) or (4) has something to be said for him. But anyone who says (2) ought to be not merely marked wrong, but penalized several points. How many? As we ask that, the 'subjective' factor rears its ugly head. The teacher must estimate the intelligence and the application the pupil has been showing, his grasp of the *whole subject*. More and more he must do that as the work he teaches rises higher above memorizing of individual elements and becomes creative understanding of a large and complex pattern of thought." [1]

Mechanical systems may suffice, after a fashion, in testing what is wholly elementary. Latin words meaning to believe, favor, help, please, and trust either take the dative or they do not, but not many of the subjects which ought to be taught to young adults in college are on this level of simplicity. All great things are complex. Instead of trying to eliminate all elements of subjectivity, the part of wisdom is to recognize the inevitability of the subjective predicament and to handle it as intelligently as possible. Our only hope lies, not in the elimination of what cannot be avoided, but in the disciplined handling of what is inevitable. The major purpose of true-false testing is fairness, but complete fairness is never achieved by this method. It merely pushes the problem back one stage. We eliminate the subjectivity of the reader, but we do not eliminate the subjective judgment of the one who sets the questions. How do we know that the judgment of the man who sets this year's alternatives is identical with that of the man who set them last year?

Our right solution of the problem of fairness cannot come by

[1] Gilbert Highet, *The Art of Teaching* (New York, 1950), p. 120.

the adoption of some academic short cut. There is no substitute for the development of wise questions which can draw out the best in a student's mind and expose weaknesses or efforts to deceive. The problem of cheating is never wholly solved by the adoption of an honor system or any other, but the problem is vastly minimized by the introduction of questions of such significance that they cannot be answered by merely looking at another student's paper. Some examiners reduce cheating markedly by providing dates or formulae and limiting the questions to matters of interpretation. By such means both competence and incompetence are truly revealed.

Rollo Walter Brown, in his memorable essay on Bliss Perry, has given the following example of Professor Perry's astute yet wonderfully fair questioning. "If you were writing to an intelligent foreigner who knew English but happened to be ignorant of the literature produced in England between 1550 and 1700, what authors or works would you chiefly recommend to him, and what reasons would you give him for your selections?" In estimating Perry's success, Brown says, "In the answers to that question it would be possible to discern all sorts of alivenesses—or deadnesses—never to be revealed by a student's check of 'True' or 'False' on a mimeographed sheet prepared by somebody else." [2] Since all who teach, and especially all who teach gladly, are more or less consciously disciples of Socrates, they cannot possibly let all of the questions be asked by others; they must develop skill in asking the questions which reveal.

It is not good enough in a college which strives to demonstrate excellence to arrange for course examinations and no more. The crucial mistake of that policy is to make the students feel that, having passed a course, they are forthwith free to forget it. The course has been "done" and checked off in the mood of the tourist who "does" Milton's cottage or Stoke Poges. The only known alternative to such fragmentation of learning is the employment of

[2] Rollo Walter Brown, "Bliss Perry," *Atlantic Monthly*, Vol. 193, p. 24.

comprehensive examinations toward the end of the student's college career. The comprehensive examination has some similarity to the great examinations which the students of English colleges face at the end, but differs markedly from anything in the English system in that it assumes prior success in course examinations. The combination of the two types is in many ways superior to either one alone.

The truly comprehensive examination has many advantages, the chief of which is the way in which the thoughtful student is likely to use his preparation for it to try to see his college education in its wholeness. Around him are his many notebooks, the papers which he has written on many subjects, and a vast accumulation of scattered ideas put down from time to time. Now his task is to pull these together and to get ready, by that means, to face mature questioning. Just as the beginning student may learn more in the week immediately prior to the course examination than in all the earlier part of the term, so likewise the advanced student, almost ready for his bachelor's degree, may learn more in getting ready for his comprehensive examination than in any other part of his college life. He must, if this is to be accomplished, be relatively free from class attendance, with plenty of time to be in the college library alone. There is a time for general conversation, but this is not it.

Unless we have comprehensive examinations and unless we take them seriously, there is really no solution of the problem presented by the person who has been clever in accumulating credits, but has no real grasp on learning. The college which stresses the comprehensive examination is saying, in no uncertain terms, that the credit system, however necessary it may be, is never sufficient. All that the credits ought to insure is the *privilege* of taking the great examination. It is a qualifying step, but no more. The general adoption of such a plan would do much to redeem American higher education in the eyes of the world, for it would insure a certain integrity.

The integrity we seek is not likely to be achieved unless the system of comprehensive examinations includes the use of outside examiners. If the senior's only inquisitors are his own beloved professors, the system is likely to be too easy. It is almost impossible to eliminate favoritism, however great the discipline of the professor concerned. But the bringing in of competent outsiders provides insurance of academic standards. It is not enough that a student merely repeat back to his instructor the instructor's own ideas and pet convictions or interpretations of events. The question is whether the professors can so equip their students that they can make a reasonable showing before scholars who have never seen them before and will probably never see them again. Only by some such means can a college have an objective check on its own standards. Otherwise the students might be ill-prepared and yet nobody ever recognize that such is the case.

The use of outside examiners is growing, but not rapidly enough. Swarthmore has long used outside scholars for the oral examinations of all who are seeking the honors degree, while Denison announces in its catalogue that every comprehensive examination shall include at least one scholar from outside the Denison faculty. The entire decision need not rest with the outsider, for he can be helped by the judgment of the one who knows the student and is aware of any special difficulties. The oral examination, in which both insiders and outsiders ask questions, is a valuable means of raising the entire level of the undertaking, but there ought to be written questions also. If visitors, including other students, are allowed to attend the oral examination, the dramatic quality of the occasion is heightened and the educational venture begins to take on some of the beneficent excitement which heretofore has been limited, for the most part, to athletics.

One striking result which comes from the introduction of outside examiners is that this practice puts the professor and the student on the same side. If there are sections in a class, and if all have the same examiner, the instructors can compete to see which section

turns in the most brilliant performance. This, however, is practically impossible when the entire outcome depends upon the same
man who is both coach and judge. It may be truly said, therefore,
that one of our real advances is that which will come when the
teacher is no longer the sole judge of his own product. This advance
can come in several ways, but one of the most practical is that of
pooling our resources in particular geographical areas. Often there
are three or four colleges of approximately equal standards within
a radius of seventy miles. These can help one another, at little
expense, by agreeing to examine each other's students, perhaps
with no exchange of money at all, but with great gain for all concerned. The colleges thus cooperating may move in the direction
of the creation of regional universities which perform their first
function in the provision of examining boards. In earlier days dis-
tance was a barrier to such a development, but it is a serious barrier no longer. This is one of the ways in which we may finally
develop a system in which we have the advantages, at the same
time, both of real colleges and of real universities. One of the best
functions of a university made up of a cluster of colleges is the
examining function, by which the maintainance of impartial
standards is assured.

If we are to make our colleges worthy of the effort they require,
we must guard the integrity of its degrees. The shame today is
that a degree may mean almost anything, even when it is designated by the same Latin words. It is not easy to dismiss the words
of the author of *The Organization Man* when he writes acidly on
this subject. "Once," he says, "the uneducated could have the
humility of ignorance. Now they are given degrees and put in
charge." [3] College catalogues are revealing mixtures. Usually, in
the early pages, noble ideals are beautifully expressed, but the
shock comes when we study the terrible proliferation of courses
which count toward that great and ancient sign of the educated

[3] W. H. Whyte, Jr., *The Organization Man* (New York: Simon and
Schuster, Inc., 1956), p. 110.

man, the bachelor of arts degree. Clifton Fadiman tells of courses in cosmetology and one in the "Humanities" which is partly devoted to the selection of socks. For such courses to have the same weight in determining a student's fitness for a degree that is given to a thorough course in logic is a manifest absurdity, yet it is done.

The whole point of a degree is that it is actually a *guarantee*. The diploma is comparable to paper money, and is therefore acceptable as academic legal tender. It is intended to mean that the outside observer can be sure that the person who lists the degree after his name has achieved a certain level of educational eminence. That is why it is called a degree. Graduation is supposed to mean something of the same thing that graduation of a thermometer indicates in the measurement of heat. In a trustworthy society we do not need to check the accuracy of every thermometer; and likewise, when a first-class college puts its sign of academic approval on a man, we do not need to inquire more carefully into his background. It ought to be evidence that he has attained a certain level of competence in the ability to think, that he feels at home in intellectual history, that he understands and practices scientific method, that he can express himself clearly in both written and oral speech, and that he is personally reliable and responsible. This may seem to be a large order, but anything less is out of line with our pretensions and our equipment. Everyone knows that thousands graduate every June who do not qualify by such a standard. That they do so is chiefly the fault of the credit system. Though there has been some improvement, the question in many colleges is not whether a young man can read and write and speak the French language, but whether he has been enrolled in a French course for two years and "passed." The crude mistake is to measure in terms of time rather than in terms of achievement.

We must decide, unequivocally, that there can be no granting of a degree except on the evidence of achievement. This is not to minimize residence, for it is by residence, as we have seen in an earlier chapter, that many of the intangibles of a college education are acquired and assimilated. Perhaps there ought to be a minimum residential requirement of three years, during which a student so comports himself that he qualifies for a test of his achievement much as he qualifies for an athletic meet. Our task is to set up an academic decathlon with perhaps ten types of achievement, all of which must be demonstrated with a minimum level of competence. It would be unreasonable, in the light of native human inequality, to demand a superior performance in everything, but there can be established a reasonable minimum without which the degree lacks both credibility and respect.

The whole idea of the degree is to keep faith with the public. Obviously the degree has no intrinsic worth; it is valuable only because of that to which it refers. And the public is being systematically deceived if a college puts its stamp of approval upon a man who is fundamentally uneducated, no matter how many years he has been enrolled at the college. The public is being deceived if the man cannot spell, if he cannot write a decent essay, if he cannot engage in abstract reasoning, if he knows nothing of modern science, if he cannot speak his own language with some understanding of grammatical structure. This last is most easily achieved by studying another language and thus seeing one's own grammar in perspective, but the question is not *how* the achievement has come about; it is *whether* it has come about. And if it has not come about, the degree is essentially spurious.

Though mention was made earlier of an academic decathlon, comparable to that of the Olympic games, the matter may be simplified by emphasis on four requirements for college graduation which, if adhered to, would recover and maintain the prestige of the bachelor's degree:

1. *Evidence of Skills.* The minimum skills are those already mentioned, such as the ability to write, to speak both privately and publicly, to use some language other than one's own, to employ mathematical symbols, and to demonstrate scientific method. In

each case, the acceptable level of competence must be determined by those already most competent in each skill. Thus the good public speaker ought to be the one to decide what is the acceptable level in his field and the good mathematician should do the same in his. Whether these skills are learned in a class or independently makes no difference at all. The question is whether they are *possessed*.

2. *General Knowledge*. Before the college can place its stamp of approval on a student, he should give evidence of such wide reading and thinking in so many fields that he at least knows what people are talking about in fields other than his own. A man does not need to be a scientist to know something of Sir Isaac Newton, nor a politician to know the multifarious work of Benjamin Franklin. If a man has a bachelor's degree and, when mention is made of Dr. Samuel Johnson, says, "Who was he?" it is reasonably certain that the degree is a shoddy one. It is not easy to determine the minimum level of competence in general knowledge, but it has to be ascertained, and that is partly what college leaders exist to decide. In any case this is the kind of achievement which outsiders expect and have a right to expect.

3. *Mastery of One Subject*. Though we do not want to go to the European university system of exclusive concentration on one field, a certain level of competence in one field is an academic necessity if superficiality is to be avoided. There is no good reason why a young person of twenty-two cannot, by careful application, know a great deal about some one thing. Indeed, in a really restricted field, he may easily know more than his professors. A young man might easily surpass his geology professor in his knowledge of a certain rock formation, and this sort of achievement would delight the professor. Unusual competence in some one area adds enormously to self-respect and this is one thing which a college ought to encourage.

4. *Evidence of Refinement*. This kind of achievement is in some ways the hardest to judge accurately, but is also the most

important. The refinement should include appreciation of both aesthetic and ethical values. It is a disgrace for a person to graduate from college with no intelligible idea of how to judge a painting or a poem, and it is even worse to graduate with no sense of moral greatness. Those who come to the end of their college days in a mood of flippancy about these matters are still sophomores and are not, accordingly, worthy of the degree. It is the task of responsible professors to know whether an adequate level has been reached in these difficult but crucial matters. If college graduates are not cultivated people, something has gone wrong in the central conception of what a college education means.

The defender of the college as it is today will be quick to reply that the college teaches all of the subjects which have been mentioned. Certainly it does, but the question is: Does the college demand competence in all these before graduation can occur? To offer is not enough. Everyone understands that the denial of degrees after four years of residence would bring pain, but Aristotle has reminded us that all education is accompanied by pain. There is disappointment when the bank clerk does not gain advancement and there is greater disappointment when the young man does not win the beautiful girl. This is of the essence of human existence. What the college must do is to make academic competition as fair and as kind as possible, but, in the end, to be firm. The firmness is not adopted for its own sake, but as the price of integrity. It is not an easy thing to sit on the examining board when a man, after years of effort, comes up for his doctor of philosophy degree, and, because it is evident that he has not arrived, to vote against him. What is still harder is to walk out of the building at the end of the session and there see the man's wife waiting to hear the news which means almost as much to her as it does to him. It is sad to think of his disappointment and of hers; but if, in order to avoid this disappointment, the committee should be tolerant of incompetence, the degree would become progressively worthless. Even now the Ph. D. degree, our highest earned degree, differs considerably in worth in different institutions. This is why some scholars put the name of the granting institutions in parentheses when they list degrees. Money is no better than the economy of the nation which issues it, and a degree is no better than the standard by which it is given.

In conclusion, it is necessary to consider briefly honorary degrees. There is no phase of our academic life more chaotic than the phase represented by these. The idea of an honorary degree is essentially a noble one. It means that a community of scholars decides to indicate its joint judgment about those who have reached the highest levels of achievement. This is noble because it eliminates entirely any consideration of the steps followed, indicating only the nature of the pinnacle that has been reached.

Splendid as the idea of the honorary degree is, it may easily be debased and its chief debasement comes by what can only be called academic inflation. The greater the number of honorary degrees that are given, the cheaper they become. The Christian colleges have erred as much as any others in this regard, particularly in giving an excessive number of doctor of divinity degrees. Some of these are extremely valuable, while others are almost worthless, but all appear the same to the public. The only answer to this problem is the answer of academic self-restraint. There are always persons who are angling for degrees, the usual method being the indirect one of working through their friends. Sometimes a degree seems to be a reward for a contribution, financial or otherwise. All of this must be resisted and is already resisted in the best colleges, for the best colleges know that the guarding of the worth of degrees, whether earned or honorary, is essential to their very life. This follows from the fact that colleges are in the civilization business, and civilization endures because of standards.

XII

The Vision of Excellence

"Moral education is impossible apart from the habitual vision of greatness."

ALFRED NORTH WHITEHEAD

A COLLEGE must, sooner or later, justify its existence. This it cannot do unless it can demonstrate some contribution to the development of a better civilization which would not otherwise be made. It must give something to men which cannot be provided by the mere printing of books or by the passing of laws. The college if it is worth keeping must show that it contributes something needful which cannot be contributed by the press, by the church, or by the technical institute.

Insofar as a college is a genuine college and not a mere credit factory, it justifies itself by the way in which it unites "the young and the old in the imaginative consideration of learning." Books have been able, ever since the popularization of printing in the middle of the fifteenth century, to impart information, but neither books nor any other impersonal duplicating device can establish for people the connection between knowledge and the zest for life. The ideal product of the American college is what Woodrow Wilson called the wholly awakened man. Because this man, when he appears, is beyond price, his appearance justifies all of the effort which the establishment and nurture of a college involves. "One Einstein or one Bohr," says Archibald MacLeish, "is worth an incalculable crop of mediocrities, whether they are designated physicists by their diplomas or not." [1] Most men will not be awakened to a full consciousness of their possibilities except by the power of imagination, of which direct confrontation with excellence is the most natural occasion. There are many features which are involved in the production of a genuine college, but all of the other features are patently insufficient if there is not some true sense in which the entire college life is an introduction to the experience of greatness. A college is an institution which, because it recognizes that the enemy is the trivial, makes a deliberate attempt, not only to create the vision of greatness, but to create it *habitually*.

Much of our present shame in both schools and colleges consists in the fact that we do not sufficiently encourage students to live up to their possibilities. Our problem is not lack of native ability, but lack of challenge. Children go along for years doing only a small fraction of what they might do and of what they would do if only the level of expectation were raised. Great mumbers of college students admit that they are coasting along during most of the weeks of the college year, employing only a small part of their native resources. Poor little papers, written at the last possible minute, are handed in by people who have the ability to write really good papers. The tragedy is the tragedy of failure to realize potentials.

That remarkable woman Edith Hamilton, who has helped so many by her books *The Greek Way*, *The Roman Way*, and *Witness to the Truth*, explains her own development by reference to the demands of her father when she was a little girl in Fort Wayne. At the age of seven, Edith Hamilton was given

[1] Archibald MacLeish, "What Is a True University?" *Saturday Review*, January 31, 1959, p. 13.

six weeks to make a full preparation of Caesar's *Gallic Wars*. Because this was expected, the girl did it. By the time she was twelve, she could read both Greek and Latin with ease, and by the time she went as a student to Bryn Mawr she already had a better training of mind than most college graduates now have. Her really splendid education has been demonstrated in all her public work. When we know how she studied, we are no longer surprised at the beautiful lucidity of her prose style. It is possible, of course, that Edith Hamilton was an unusually gifted child, but she does not think so. What she thinks is that, in spite of some bad teaching, she was encouraged to live somewhere near the fullness of her powers. When we realize how many persons of equal powers are now being ruined by low standards of expectation, we know that our contemporary practice involves a greater waste of human resources than we can afford to bear.

Few contemporary developments are more disquieting than that represented by the cult of mediocrity. The heart of this mediocrity is deliberate limitation of achievement. It is a terrible and frightening thing when it appears in industrial establishments, but it is far more frightening when it appears in educational establishments. It appears in educational establishments whenever the tyranny of the majority is such that young people feel pressure not to excel. The persecution of the individual who has the courage to learn and to produce at full capacity may be carried on in numerous subtle ways or it may be overt. Many students do shoddy work for the simple reason that they are ashamed to do their best and thereby make an implicit criticism of their unambitious fellows.

It makes little difference how advanced our technology is if the ideal of excellence is lost in our civilization. When it is lost, men and women habitually settle for what is passing; they put in the time; they hold the job. The shame, then, is that they have nothing in their experience of which they may be justifiably proud. There are many ways in which civilizations decline, but this is one of the most obvious ways. If the colleges do not provide an antidote to mediocrity, it is hard to know where such an antidote will be found.

Our trouble lies not in any particular curriculum or in any particular method of teaching, but in our basic philosophy. The heart of this philosophy is centered in a special conception of democracy. As usually happens in human experience, the best and the worst are separated only by a thin line. If by democracy we mean a system of thought and action, according to which every person, regardless of his family or racial origin or economic condition, is allowed to develop his powers and to take his fair share of responsibility in public life, then democracy is something good indeed. Whatever its dangers, it is certainly superior to a system of tyranny or even a system of hereditary privilege. But if, as a result of subtle but crucial changes in the idea, democracy means a system in which we glorify the common at the expense of the uncommon man, it becomes mediocrity and leads inevitably to cultural decay. Since both strains have always been present, at least potentially, in western life, it has been easy to confuse them and nowhere has it been easier than in education.

The damaging kind of democracy has been with us in the American experiment for a long time and has sometimes been noted by astute observers. Seventy years ago Matthew Arnold recognized and described the danger of low standards implicit in the leveling kind of democracy, which honors too greatly the common man, to the neglect of real excellence. The leveling tendency he called "the Anglo-Saxon contagion," a contagion which he saw as something associated unnecessarily with what was valid in the democratic life. The wheat and the tares, it seemed to him, were growing together. "Whatever one may think of the general danger to the world from the Anglo-Saxon contagion," he wrote in his essay on Milton, "it appears to me difficult to deny that the growing greatness and influence of the United States does bring with it some danger to the ideal of a high and rare excellence. The *average man* is too much a religion there; his performance is unduly magnified, his shortcomings are not duly seen and admitted." [2]

What we sometimes forget, in our glorification of democracy, is that democracy has not really succeeded in producing the good life, except as it has been combined with the recognition of aristocracy, particularly the aristocracy of merit rather than that arising from the accident of birth. Benjamin Franklin was born into a poor and modest family, but he was certainly an aristocrat because he was one of the best.[3] He stood like an intellectual giant among his Philadelphia neighbors of the eighteenth-century. Much of the success of the American system of government stems from the fact that America had, at the crucial moment of her history, a galaxy of men comparable to Franklin in stature. Our plan of government rests, not on the ideas of average men, but on the ideas of the men who composed the Mayflower Compact and Penn's Plan of Government and the thoughts of Thomas Jefferson. Nearly all of the men who gathered in Independence Hall in July, 1776, were aristocratic in a deep and true sense of the word. They read great books; they lived disciplined lives; they maintained elevated standards of personal conduct; they were men of good education and of constructive thought. It would not have been surprising if men of such unusual ability had taken advantage of their positions of leadership to perpetuate family privilege and to give peculiar advantages to their descendents, but this is what they rejected as unworthy. Many expected Washington to become a monarch. The remarkable thing is that the

[2] Matthew Arnold, *Essays in Criticism* (London: Macmillan and Company, Ltd., 1902), p. 57.

[3] In the words of George Wharton Pepper, Franklin was "the most civilized man of his day." His was the only name signed to four great documents: the Declaration of Independence, the Treaty of Alliance with France, the Treaty of Peace with Great Britain, and the Constitution of the United States.

aristocrats were also democrats. They believed in a third alternative, as far from special privilege, on the one hand, as from the
glorification of the average, on the other. Influenced by Plato,
they proposed to set up, not a mere democracy, but a Republic.
Like Plato they expected to combine democracy of opportunity
with aristocracy of ability, of achievement, and of responsibility.
They hoped to give every man a chance to show his powers and
then to give the greatest recognition to those with the greatest
powers. The kind of democracy they espoused was not that which
involves the patent falsehood that all men are equal. All, wrote
Jefferson, are "created equal," which is an entirely different matter.
What this means is that all, regardless of differences in native
powers, are children of the Divine Father and all, in consequence,
are to be accorded the dignity which derives from the Divine
Paternity. Men, thought the founding fathers, are equal in fundamental origin, but vastly unequal in abilities, in willingness to
work, and in the acceptance of responsibility.

Much of the danger in our current philosophy of education
has come by the glorification of the democratic aspects of our
life without an equal glorification of the aristocratic aspects, without which the former can lead to decay. An English woman who
has been an exchange teacher in America put her finger on this
point, with the advantage of her outside view, before she returned
home. "I think," she wrote, "many Americans have deluded themselves into believing that the same kind of education is necessary for all in order to achieve educational equality of opportunity." [4] The emphasis on equality can be so made that it mili-
tates against *quality*. That this emphasis is made and deliberately
made is beyond doubt, and it is made in the light of a supposed
ideal, that of a special form of togetherness or collectivity. Differences are consequently minimized at both ends of the scale.
On the one end, parents are warned against encouraging their

[4] Ivy Cooper-Marsh, "Putting Equality First in School," *London Daily
Telegraph*, May 20, 1958.

able children to get ahead of the class; while, on the other, the inept and lazy are advanced along with their comrades, just as though they were successful students.

Because ideas have consequences, the false conception of democracy makes an important difference in practice. The pressure of conformity is so powerful and so pervasive that students of promise, afraid of seeming queer, refuse to accomplish all that is possible. How, if this is our standard mentality, are we to produce in sufficient numbers, the leaders of thought and action which our generation so sorely needs? We need intellectual aristocrats in our democracy almost as much as we needed them when our system of government was being formed. In short, we need uncommon men who are adept at the task of sustaining a republic as others were adept at inventing it.

The place to begin in our educational philosophy is a change in purpose. We must make our goal, not adjustment, and not even happiness, but excellence. We may, indeed, achieve happiness in this way, but the happiness will come as a by-product rather than something at which we have directly aimed. Young people who begin to have a taste of what excellence in performance and production may mean often discover that this brings a joy and satisfaction which are not known in mediocrity, no matter how much entertainment is provided. Though many students of today do not know it by experience, the truth is that the joy to be found in writing a good essay, striving for genuine competence rather than for a passing grade, is a great joy. This is because man is made to be a producer. We are happy when we *make*, and we are happiest when we make at the level of excellence.

Such a philosophy of education requires a radical shift in emphasis. It means that we must not hesitate to bring young people into contact with what is difficult and challenging. It means that we shall divide students by levels of achievement. The great ideas must be presented, not in a watered-down version, but in the finest form which each group is able to comprehend. It may not be easy to read and understand the works of Immanuel Kant, but that is no adequate reason for avoiding them in college. If others have been able to comprehend, so can we. The famous Richard Baxter of Kidderminster said in his *Autobiography* that he made it a habit to preach once a year over the heads of his congregation, thus to keep them in their place and to show them what he could do if he would. It is good, as Baxter knew, for people, at some times in their lives, to have to stretch.

It is good to meditate on the uses of greatness. The powerful influence of great men is that, by their very existence and by our knowledge of that existence, they can shake us out of our complacency. Thus one of the truly wonderful experiences of living in the twentieth century is the sense of lift that comes from being alive at the same time as Sir Winston Churchill. To go straight through his six-volume history of *The Second World War* is to encounter the vision of excellence at first hand. Here are great issues, great decisions, great words, and great deeds. Many of the decisions have affected the welfare of millions. It is literally possible that apart from Churchill's indomitable will and intelligent judgment, Adolf Hitler might still be alive and victorious, still enforcing his will on millions of unfortunate people. The elimination of this threat was not something that was inevitable; it came only because of what particular men thought and suffered and accomplished.

Education, if it is sound, will insure the encounter with greatness at as many points as possible. It is good for the young life to measure itself in contrast to the prophets of Israel or Socrates or Julius Caesar or Oliver Cromwell or Benjamin Franklin or Abraham Lincoln and many more. A great part of the value of the classic tradition in education inheres in the fact that the student is nearly always forced to recognize the existence of first-rate intelligence. He may not appreciate it all, and sometimes he is bogged down in syntax or vocabulary, but the words he is translating are the words as actually written down by Cicero and Vir-

gil and their kind. He is living every day with people who are
nobler than he is, and there is always a chance of his being un-
conciously influenced by this experience.

When the practice of learning great things by heart began to
decline is really hard to say, but there is no doubt that the decline
has come. Thousands now in colleges cannot repeat *anything* from
memory, neither Scripture nor poetry nor anything else. The loss
involved in this failure is incalculable. It means that the conscious
sources of beauty and meaning are far fewer and weaker than they
need to be. The case for learning great literature by heart is made
by Sir Richard Livingstone in the following sentences:

In education, as in life, we are formed by our atmosphere without
knowing it. We store up unconsciously spiritual tissue of whose nature and importance we are unaware. Later we may come to know
and appreciate the influences that have formed us. For the mind is
like a garden. Seeds are scattered on the soil and most are lost, but
some lie inert till the outside influence of sun and moisture wakes
them to activity. That is a parable of education. It scatters ideas and
information on the surface of the mind; much perishes forgotten,
but some seeds lie dormant till the quickening power of experience
brings them to life. Hence the value of a practice too much neglected
in modern education, the habit of learning great literature by heart
and so storing up a treasure which later life may enable us to use.[5]

As everyone knows, the right time to learn literature by heart
is early youth. George Foot Moore claimed that all of his great store
of this kind was fastened in his mind before the age of ten. Certainly a child of that age should be able to repeat the finest of
the Psalms, Lincoln's Gettysburg Address, some passages from
Shakespeare's plays, and some famous sonnets, as well as lesser
productions. Once thousands could repeat considerable passages
from Longfellow and Whittier. But what are we to do if we have
a college generation in which this great principle of education has
been neglected or ignored or even opposed? The answer is that

[5] Sir Richard Livingstone, *The Future in Education* (Cambridge, Eng.:
Cambridge University Press, 1941), p. 24.

it is never too late to learn. If college people have been cheated of their rightful intellectual heritage in their early years, appropriate steps must be taken to restore the heritage in early maturity. A college student willing to set himself to the task can fill his mind with productions of great minds far more rapidly than he realizes. Almost any adult can learn to repeat a sonnet in an hour and, with a few repetitions, have it secure for the remainder of his life. Then he can have it as a standard of reference by which the addiction to the trivial can be judged and seen in its true light. We know how low the lowlands are only by contrasting them with the distant hills.

However much we may try, we cannot revive a classical education in its earlier form, and to do so would not be desirable even if it were possible. The old education, based almost entirely on the works of Greece and Rome, had merit, but it also had great weaknesses. Even Dr. Arnold never introduced the study of natural science at Rugby and the only teaching of modern history was confined to one hour a week which the Doctor handled himself. The system produced strong and wise men, but it is not the only way of producing strength and wisdom. The virtue of the system lay not in constant translation from dead languages, but rather in the production of the vision of greatness, both in the character of the teachers and in the treasures so laboriously unearthed. This is something we require today, and if we are not going to get it in the old way, we must get it in some other way.

One of the best methods is that of studying the Greek writers in translation. Without denying the value of the hard work of digging it out alone, it remains true that the student may get more out of a translation than he can get from the original be- cause, in studying a good translation, he can soon feel the entire sweep of the movement. A contemporary student ought not to be denied an acquaintance with some of the greatest minds of all history just because he has never learned to read the Greek language. These minds constitute an intellectual acropolis, to

which any contemporary student can look up with profit. Even
one semester spent in studying the works of Aeschylus, Sophocles,
and Euripides, with Aristophanes thrown in for balance, can be a
time of singular revelation. There is nothing wrong with a method
which makes use of great translations.[6] After all, most people
who read the Hebrew Scriptures read them in modern-language
translations and not in the Hebrew. Why should we not follow,
in dealing with Xenophon and his famous contemporaries, the
same pattern that we follow in dealing with Isaiah and his
contemporaries?

It is not surprising that so many generations in periods of
self-dissatisfaction, such as we now experience, have turned
to Greece in its noblest period. They turn there, not primarily
because of a language, but because of a pattern of life. Greek
literature, especially in its treatments of politics and ethics,
contains an antidote to acceptance of either corruption or mediocrity in public life. Plato's warnings about the dangers of
democracy, as found in the eighth book of the *Republic*, are
strikingly relevant to our contemporary situation. Both Plato
and Aristotle, in spite of their manifest differences in political
theory, present a view of life in which morals are part of
politics and politics part of morals. A student who gets out of
college without the encouragement to study the major Platonic
dialogues and at least the first four books of Aristotle's *Ethics*
may rightly claim that he has been mistreated. He will not, of
course, end with these, for there are potential encounters with
excellence in connection with later and contemporary minds,
but a genuine appreciation of the best minds of classic Greece
is almost certain to create a mood of enduring dissatisfaction
with the second-rate.

If Greece provides one of the two major sources of the

6 Whitehead says, "I prefer a translation of what a Greek actually said, to
any talk about the Greeks, written by an Englishman, however well he has
done it." *The Aims of Education* (New York, 1929), p. 114.

spiritual life of the West, Palestine provides the other. This ancient and tragic land has put us so greatly in its debt that the debt can never be paid. It is fearful to think what contemporary life might be if the redemptive influences which come from the Hebrew heritage and the Christian Scriptures were lacking. When we think how the words of the Bible have influenced even those who have never read a word of it, and the way in which the Biblical influence has affected our entire culture, we realize how preposterous it is to claim to give an adequate modern education when all reference to this is omitted. It is not only that, as was pointed out earlier, most of the higher education of America began with a religious incentive; there is also the point that the Palestinian contribution has affected our form of government, our Declaration of Independence, our social services, and our fundamental standards of conduct. It is no adequate answer to say that we do not live up perfectly to these standards. Neither did the ancient Hebrews, as any reader of the Old Testament can easily verify, and neither did the early Christians or the Christians of any period. It is precisely because we fail so often that the standard is our priceless possession. If we did not have a standard by which to judge, we should not even be aware of failure.

No student can understand his own culture merely by studying the contemporary fruits; he must also know the roots. This is why the Great Books movement put into its plan of reading an early acquaintance with the story of Naboth's Vineyard. The modern student is rightly interested in such conceptions as equality before the law, due process, and the dignity of the individual, but he will understand these far better if he knows how and where they arose and how they have been developed. Still more important is it to understand and to appreciate a view of life and reality in conformance with which these great conceptions can make sense. Commenting upon the Biblical account of Naboth and his famous vineyard, a contemporary philosopher says something which it would be good for every student to know.

Thus the commoner has rights, so clear-cut and so well established that not even the king can override them. Remember who the king was: supreme authority, military, civil, political, and religious. No law should be able to stop him, for he is the law. That the crown can do no wrong is still preserved as a legal principle in a great commonwealth, though it be treated as a legal fiction in most cases today. It was no legal fiction in the Oriental kingdom. The king was legislature, judiciary, and executive; and the Lord's anointed as well, who could make and unmake high priests. But in the little kingdom of Palestine this absolute monarch's power is limited by the commoner's inalienable rights.[7]

To know the Bible, with the aid of scholarly insight and excellent instruction, ought to be the privilege of every advanced student. If he faces openly and humbly the succession of the prophets of Israel, noting how Isaiah and Micah built upon their great predecessors, Amos and Hosea, while they in turn provided foundations for their successors, such as Jeremiah and Ezekiel, he is bound to be deeply impressed, and he may find the basis of his own life strengthened. He will stand in amazement at the fact that a little people could do so much, and that a physically feeble nation could survive while the strong ones perished. In like manner he can be immensely enriched by the Epistles and Gospels and Acts of the New Testament, finding that a scholarly approach need not destroy appreciation, but is more likely to insure its enlargement.

Though the purpose of a college is intellectual rather than evangelical, an education in a land so deeply affected by Jesus Christ is obviously lacking if knowledge of Christ is left out. It is odd for people who date every letter and document from Christ's birth to know nothing of importance about Him.

[7] Gregory Vlastos, *Christian Faith and Democracy* (New York: Association Press, 1947), pp. 16, 17.

The point of central importance in Christianity is Christ Himself. Any humble seeker of any faith or of no faith can profit by a careful study of the fourfold portrait which the Gospels provide. If it is the habitual vision of greatness that we require, here it is. We can read today how He lived, how He taught, how He attracted some and alienated others, how He healed, how He nourished a little fellowship of men remarkably like ourselves, and how He was executed by the Roman authorities.

The author of *The Imitation of Christ* speaks for a multitude of obscure persons when, in the first chapter of the first book, he writes, "Let our foremost resolve be to meditate on the life of Jesus Christ." A Christian is one whose life is changed by this experience.

How can any person claim to be educated and to participate intelligently in what is, in part, a Christian civilization if he has never seen Christ as His contemporaries saw Him in Galilee and Judea, if he has never weighed carefully the convincement of the men who were closest to Him and knew Him best, and if he has never tried to understand the conviction that "God was in Christ, reconciling the world unto Himself"? "That conviction of a few Jewish peasants in a minor dependency of the great and highly civilized Roman Empire seemed to most of its citizens an extravagant folly, but their fellowship persisted as the Empire, apparently so stable and permanent, fell into collapse, and subsequently outlived every other creed and philosophy of the Graeco-Roman world." [8] Whatever else a good education does, it develops a respect for facts, and what has just been said, in Livingstone's words, is undoubtedly a fact. Anyone who means seriously to wrestle with the mystery of existence must make an effort to react reasonably to such a fact. The nature of the reaction is the inalienable privilege of the individual student. The responsibility of the college is to give him a chance to be aware of what the fact is.

[8] Livingstone, *The Future in Education*, p. 125.

It is not the duty of a college to teach everything, but it is the duty of the college to teach well all that it does teach. A professor of science who never says a word about ethics, yet who demonstrates daily his disdain of shoddy work and fragmentary preparation, may in fact be engaged deeply in the ethical task. How can the shallow young man be reached who admits that his only interest is in some kind of degree, a well-paid job, and a late model car? This is not easy and certainly there is no recipe for success in every case. But sometimes young people of even this degree of shallowness are aroused, and when they are, it is usually because some professor has maintained such a high standard of quality in his scientific or literary or artistic work that the student has been shocked by the contrast between this and his own triviality. Sometimes the revolutionary vision comes not by a religious sermon so much as by a confrontation with hitherto unknown beauty. "There are few better ways of serving God," says Professor George Hedley, "than in the creating of objects and sounds of beauty to declare his praise." [9]

It is because we cannot expect the desired change to occur once for all that the vision must be "habitual." There is in education what has been called the law of delayed action, which means that influences sometimes have a real effect, though the effect appears at a later date. Almost every teacher has the experience of saying something, near the end of a course, which suddenly strikes fire. A student breaks in and says, "That's grand. Why didn't you say that before? It would have made everything clear." The professor is invariably forced to answer, "I *did* say it, but you were not then able to hear." This does not mean that the saying, on the earlier occasion, was wasted. The seed was all of the time getting ready to germinate. The best fruits of any work are the fruits we never see. In countless cases a group of graduates will get together and remind each

[9] George Hedley, *Religion on the Campus* (New York, 1955), p. 24.

other of some high moment in some class, though the man most responsible for the high moment seldom knows that it has been even appreciated. But it is not necessary that he should know, for it is more important to have the growth occur than to be aware of its occurrence. The matter of credit is not a matter of first importance.

It is a fortunate fact that the powerful effect of the encounter with excellence can come through the instrumentality of essentially modest persons. Sometimes the instrument is a teacher, sometimes it is another student, sometimes it is a book. All that the human instrument needs is enough potential greatness to appreciate true greatness. A man who cannot produce light can nevertheless make a window to let the light shine through and thereby come into places that would otherwise be dark. The English professor may not be able to preach a brilliant and moving sermon, but he may be able, instead, to help someone to read Shakespeare with understanding. If so, he is thereby making a step forward in the moral progress of the race. He is doing this because the enemy is the trivial and because acquaintance with Shakespeare inevitably involves high seriousness as well as excellent comedy. It is hard to be complacently mediocre again, once we have met with something which is really well done. There are many ways of making a better world, a world in which men are more sensitive and more honest and more compassionate, but the most effective way is direct confrontation with whatever involves essential dignity.[10]

The task of the college is to point to the undoubted excellence that has occurred in the human venture in the hope that it may be repeated and surpassed. The colleges, if they could see their vocation in these high terms, might make a tremendous difference. There are moments of opportunity, and ours

[10] This is the point of the magnificent text, "Finally, brethren, whatsoever things are true, whatsoever things are honest, whatsoever things are just, whatsoever things are pure, whatsoever things are lovely, whatsoever things are of good report . . . think on these things" (Philippians 4:8).

may be one of them. It is highly revealing to know that after years and probably centuries in which no human being ran a mile in less than four minutes, the four-minute mark was broken forty-five times in four years. Something like this could occur in our intellectual life, as it certainly did occur in the life of Athens in the fifth and fourth centuries B.C., and as it happened in the Renaissance. To contemplate the century of genius covering the lives of Galileo and Newton and so many more in natural science, philosophy, and letters is really inspiring. Why should this not come again? We shall not change human nature, but it is part of the meaning of human nature that it involves untold and usually undeveloped possibilities of both good and ill. We have great and terrible problems, but a generation that could produce atomic fission and launch earth satellites is not exactly decadent.

Professor Hardin Craig has given us a stimulating lesson in what is possible when a serious effort is made to raise the sights of an academic community. He gave and prepared a convocation address at the University of North Carolina which moved the students so deeply that there was a noticeable difference, even in the grade-point average of the total university in the next term. Professor Craig's theme was "Renaissance Now," with constant emphasis on the kind of excellence that can be appreciated and partly demonstrated by contemporary students, and that will be demonstrated if they really try. For some, the effect of the wise man's eloquence no doubt wore off, but there are others who, as a result of what Professor Craig said, are different to this day. Something of this kind could occur in our entire nation, but it will not occur unless colleges take the lead both in precept and example. It is the colleges, more than any other institutions, which must provide constant reminders of the difference between greatness and mere grandeur or bigness. The specter which haunts us is that of triviality in the houses of grandeur. We cannot produce, on order, human beings of the caliber of Churchill or Einstein or Wilson, but there is something that we can do, if we will. We can provide an atmosphere in which some people of potential worth will develop powers which otherwise would never have been recognized even by those who possess them.

John Milton, whose noble words on education have provided a guide for so many, lived in the very heart of one century of genius, and now may, if we listen, help us to produce another. His vision of the possibility is still so relevant that it has been emblazoned around the walls of the great hall at the University of Toronto: "Methinks I see in my mind a noble and puissant nation rousing herself like a strong man after sleep, and shaking her invincible locks." Such words are appropriate to the life of a college because the college exists to help to make them come true. The deepest reason for a college is an unrealized ideal. What inspires her men and women is the vision of a society of learning and teaching and pioneering that continues to be a community of understanding whatever the prejudice and confusion of the surrounding world. Because men are imperfect creatures, this vision is never wholly achieved, even by the good college, but it is this vision which provides the college with a reason for being. It is her most precious possession.

A Select Bibliography

BARZUN, JACQUES, *Teacher in America*, New York, 1944.

BROWN, KENNETH K., *Not Minds Alone*, New York, 1954.

CUNINGHAM, CHARLES E., *Timothy Dwight, 1752–1817*, New York, 1942.

GRUENINGER, JOHN PAUL VON (ed). *Toward a Christian Philosophy of Higher Education*, Philadelphia, 1957.

HEDLEY, GEORGE, *Religion on the Campus*, New York, 1955.

HIGHET, GILBERT, *The Art of Teaching*, New York, 1950.

JACOB, PHILIP E., *Changing Values in College*, New York, 1957.

LeFEVRE, PERRY, *The Christian Teacher*, New York, 1958.

LIVINGSTONE, SIR RICHARD, *Education for a World Adrift*, Cambridge, 1943.

————, *The Future in Education*, Cambridge, 1941.

LOWRY, HOWARD, *The Mind's Adventure*, Philadelphia, 1950.

NASH, ARNOLD, *The University and the Modern World*, New York, 1944.

NEWMAN, JOHN HENRY, *The Idea of a University*, London, 1929.

PERRY, BLISS, *And Gladly Teach*, Boston, 1935.

ROMEIN, TUNIS, *Education and Responsibility*, Lexington, University of Kentucky Press, 1955.

SWARTHMORE COLLEGE FACULTY, *An Adventure in Education*, New York, 1941.

TEAD, ORDWAY, *Character Building and Higher Education*, New York, 1953.

————, *The Climate of Learning*, New York, 1958.

WHITE, LYNN T. JR., *Educating Our Daughters.* New York, 1950.

WHITEHEAD, ALFRED NORTH, *The Aims of Education and Other Essays*, New York, 1929.

WILSON, WOODROW, *The Public Papers of Woodrow Wilson*, New York, 1925.

Index of Names

Acton, Lord, 38
Adams, John, 8, 152
Aeschylus, 191
Amherst College, 6, 8, 23 n
Amos, 193
Andrewes, Lancelot, 107
Aristophanes, 191
Aristotle, 35, 84, 89, 100, 191
Arnold, Matthew, 184, 185
Arnold, Dr. Thomas, 80, 190
Augustine, Saint, 25

Barker, Ernest, 84, 85
Barnard College, 80, 114
Baruch, Bernard, 77
Barzun, Jacques, 44
Baxter, Richard, 188
Becker, Carl L., 22, 48
Blanshard, Brand, 81, 106
Boas, George, 102
Bohr, Niels, 182
Boston University, 160 n
Bradley, F. H., 153 n
Brown, Rollo Walter, 114, 172
Bryce, Lord, 59
Bryn Mawr, 10, 80, 113
Burke, Edmund, 161
Buttrick, George A., 21 n

Calhoun, Robert L., 72, 109
Carver, George Washington, 65
Cambridge University, 116
Centre College, 114, 145
Christ, 17, 24, 28, 30, 194
Churchill, Sir Winston, 40, 188, 198
Cicero, 188

Clark, William, 32
Coe College, 89
Columbia University, 34, 114
Conant, James Bryant, 10
Cooper-Marsh, Ivy, 186 n
Craig, Hardin, 197
Cromwell, Oliver, 188
Cuningham, Charles E., 47 n

Danforth Foundation, 31
Dante, 96
Davidson College, 55, 152
Descartes, Rene, 157 n
Dirks, J. Edward, 31
Duke University, 114, 141
Dwight, Timothy, 46, 47, 55, 139, 140

Earlham College, x
Einstein, Albert, 182, 198
Eliot, T. S., 107
Emerson, Ralph Waldo, 17, 91, 107
Euripides, 191
Ezekiel, 193

Fadiman, Clifton, 176
Frankfurter, Felix, 99
Franklin, Benamin, 51, 178, 185, 188
Freud, Sigmund, 25

Gabriel, Ralph Henry, 47 n
Galen, 90
Galileo, 197
George Williams College, 157 n
Gettell, Richard Glenn, 128, 129
Gildersleeve, Basil L., 12

201

Index of Subjects

Ability to judge, 13
Academic tenure, 46
Administrators, 63
Admission officers, 54, 71
Adult education, 158 f
Advanced study, 7 n
Alumni, 60 f
American universities, 6
Art of teaching, 34
Athletics, 145–150
Attendance at class, 93
Auxiliary enterprises, 24

Beauty, creation of, 195
Biblical heritage, 29, 193
Board members, 73 ff
Bookstore, 57
Business, 100

Children, responsibility to, 162–164
Christian college, the, 17
Christian influence, 192–194
Christian perspective, 24
Christian philosophy, 24
Christian university, 27
Civilization, price of, 102
Class conflict, 69
Classics, 89 f
College chapel, 28, 139–144
College in American life, 9, 16
Coeducation, 115 ff
Commitment, 37, 72
Committee work, 45
Community, 72 f, 150
Community service, 124
Competitive coexistence, 59, 167

Complexity of a woman's life, 118, 123
Comprehensive examinations, 173
Coordinate education, 114–116
Cost of education, 51
Counseling, 91 f, 126
Credit system, 92 f

Degrees, value of, 3, 166, 175, 177
Democracy, dangers of, 184–187, 191
Detachment, 22
Dialectical materialism, 26
Dialogue, 42
Dignity, 109
Dining in college, 133 ff
Discussions, 42
Doctor's degrees, 180

Elective system, 81–83
Engineering, 95, 99
European university, 6, 101
Evening centers, 158
Examinations, 167–175
Examination, College Board, 53
Excellence, ideal of, 183, 196
Expansion, danger of, 48, 78
Expenditures, 154

Family House, 126
Fear of friendship, 58
Feminism, 113, 117
Financial problem, 70, 77
Forced spread, 83
Fraternities and sororities, 136–139
Freedom and responsibility, 26
Freshman teaching, 88

Set in Linotype Electra
Format by Marguerite Swanton
Manufactured by The Riverside Press
Published by HARPER & BROTHERS, *New York*